Agatha Heterodyne & the Siege of Mechanicsburg

A Gaslamp Fantasy with Adventure, Romance & Mad Science

Story by Kaja & Phil Foglio
Drawings by Phil Foglio
Colors by Cheyenne Wright

OTHER BOOKS FROM AIRSHIP ENTERTAINMENT AND STUDIO FOGLIO

Girl Genius® Graphic Novels

Girl Genius Volume One:
Agatha Heterodyne and the Beetleburg Clank

Girl Genius Volume Two:
Agatha Heterodyne and the Airship City

Girl Genius Volume Three:
Agatha Heterodyne and the Monster Engine

Girl Genius Volume Four:
Agatha Heterodyne and the Circus of Dreams

Girl Genius Volume Five:
Agatha Heterodyne and the Clockwork Princess

Girl Genius Volume Six:
Agatha Heterodyne and the Golden Trilobite

Girl Genius Volume Seven:
Agatha Heterodyne and the Voice of the Castle

Girl Genius Volume Eight:
Agatha Heterodyne and the Chapel of Bones

Girl Genius Volume Nine:
Agatha Heterodyne and the Heirs of the Storm

Girl Genius Volume Ten:
Agatha Heterodyne and the Guardian Muse

Girl Genius Volume Eleven:
Agatha Heterodyne and the Hammerless Bell

Girl Genius® Novels

Girl Genius: Agatha H. and the Airship City

Girl Genius: Agatha H. and the Clockwork Princess

Girl Genius® is published by:
Airship Entertainment™: a happy part of Studio Foglio, LLC
2400 NW 80th St #129 Seattle WA 98117-4449, USA

Please visit our Web sites at www.airshipbooks.com and www.girlgenius.net

Story by Phil & Kaja Foglio. Pencils by Phil Foglio. Colors by Cheyenne Wright. Selected spot illustrations colored by Kaja Foglio and/or Cheyenne Wright. Logos, Lettering, Artist Bullying & Book Design by Kaja. Fonts mostly by Comicraft– www.comicbookfonts.com.

This material originally appeared from November 2011 to December 2012 at www.girlgenius.net.

Published simultaneously in Hardcover (ISBN 978-1-890856-58-8) and Softcover (ISBN 978-1-890856-57-1) editions.

First Printing: August 2013 PRINTED IN THE USA

We would like to dedicate this volume to the men and women of the United States Postal Service, who have patiently delivered hundreds of thousands of copies of Girl Genius to readers for over a decade with hardly any problems…at least, none worth mentioning. Thank you for a job well done!
In particular, we would like to single out the staff of the Ballard Station (98107); Rod, Ken, Bob, Dean, Rosalie, Linda, Peter, & Gerry, who had to deal with us personally, and yet always managed to look happy to see us.
Thanks for that, too.

Phil Foglio

Co–chair of Transylvania Polygnostic University's Department of Very Nearly True History. Chevalier of the Most Exalted Order of Storytellers, Raconteurs and Yarn–Spinners (junior division). Hereditary Keeper of the Indestructible Lizard. Liar First Class as Recognized by the Society of Fabulists, Buskers, Diviners and Technical Scribes. Toadeater Third Class for the Mechanicsburg Young Minions & Lab Rats Adventure Club.

Kaja Foglio

Co–chair of Transylvania Polygnostic University's Department of Very Nearly True History. Three-time winner of the Hyrulian Dueling Society's Annual Quest for the Princess and Pig Hunt. Vice President of the Survival Under Extreme Duress Inner Circle of the Adventure Society. Grand Dame of the Ladies' Atelier for Social Mores and Beverage Appreciation. Occupier of the Department of Humorous Misunderstandings' Hit–The–Ground–Running Chair for T.P.U.'s Hypatia of Alexandria College.

Cheyenne Wright

King of the Most Glorious Subterranean Nation of Daarkstone (abdicated). High Protector of the Heir Apparent. Doctor of Non–Euclidian Physics. Master of Blasphemous Wavelengths for the Society of Dark Light, Non–Lethal Radiation, and Mysterious Rays. First Dan of the Zen Painting Society, and Chairman of the Color Appreciation Through Echolocation Society.

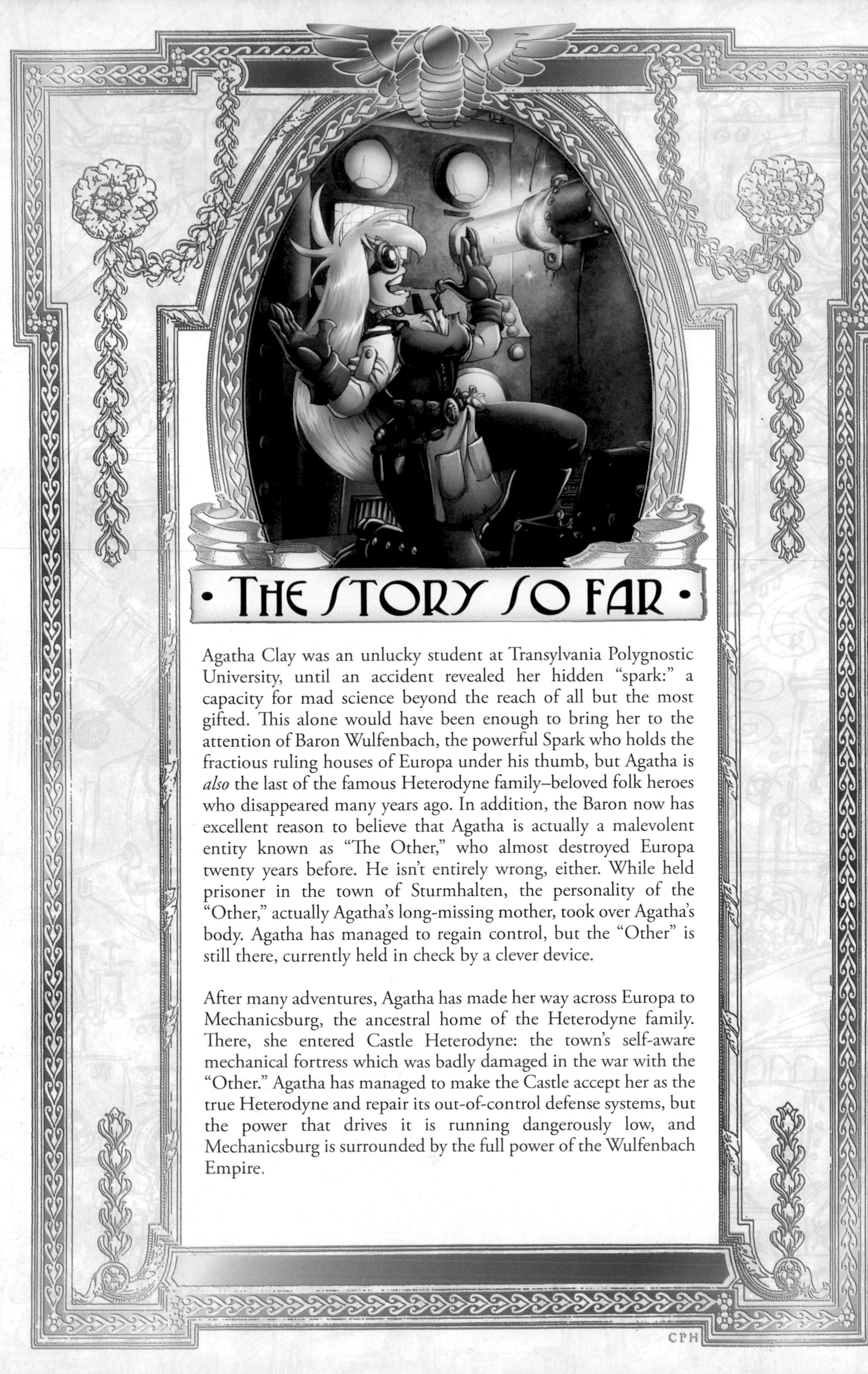

• The Story So Far •

Agatha Clay was an unlucky student at Transylvania Polygnostic University, until an accident revealed her hidden "spark:" a capacity for mad science beyond the reach of all but the most gifted. This alone would have been enough to bring her to the attention of Baron Wulfenbach, the powerful Spark who holds the fractious ruling houses of Europa under his thumb, but Agatha is *also* the last of the famous Heterodyne family–beloved folk heroes who disappeared many years ago. In addition, the Baron now has excellent reason to believe that Agatha is actually a malevolent entity known as "The Other," who almost destroyed Europa twenty years before. He isn't entirely wrong, either. While held prisoner in the town of Sturmhalten, the personality of the "Other," actually Agatha's long-missing mother, took over Agatha's body. Agatha has managed to regain control, but the "Other" is still there, currently held in check by a clever device.

After many adventures, Agatha has made her way across Europa to Mechanicsburg, the ancestral home of the Heterodyne family. There, she entered Castle Heterodyne: the town's self-aware mechanical fortress which was badly damaged in the war with the "Other." Agatha has managed to make the Castle accept her as the true Heterodyne and repair its out-of-control defense systems, but the power that drives it is running dangerously low, and Mechanicsburg is surrounded by the full power of the Wulfenbach Empire.

CPH

GREAT VULCAN ON A VELOCIPEDE
IT'S STEAMCON'S AIRSHIP AWARD FOR GIRL GENIUS!
Potpourri:
Studio Foglio
THANK YOU, STEAMCON II MEMBERS!

DEEP UNDER CASTLE HETERODYNE—
THE GREAT MOVEMENT CHAMBER
NOW, FOR THE LAST TIME—
PULL!
CLICK! CLICK! CLICK! CLICK! CLICK! CLICK! CLICK! CLICK! CLICK! CLICK! CLICK! CLICK!
CREEEAK!
ALMOST...
ARGH!
CLUNK
COME ON...A LITTLE TO THE LEFT, YOU MISERABLE PIECE OF KLUDGE—
LEFT! LEFT!
SHONK!
THAT DID IT!
IT'S IN!

CLA-
KLAK!

KUNK
KUNK-
KUNK

KUNK
KUNK
KUNKUNKUNK
YEAH! IT'S GOING!

HEY, CASTLE!

YOU HEAR THAT, YOU STUPID PILE OF ROCKS?
IT'S ALL FIXED!
YOUR POWER'S BACK ON!
AH! WELL DONE, HERR VON ZINZER!

AND JUST IN TIME...
DOO
AAAH!

TCH.
WELL, YOU'LL GET USED TO IT. HEH.
THE MINIONS ALWAYS DO...

JUST OUTSIDE MECHANICSBURG— THE FLAGSHIP OF THE HELIOLUX AIRSHIP FLEET...
...IT'S STOPPED.
WHAT? WHAT DO YOU MEAN IT'S STOPPED?
THEY WERE IN MID-SENTENCE!
WULFENBACH AIRSHIP ACCURSED DRAGON—YOU ARE CLEARED FOR DOCKING.
LIEUTENANT HAGOPIA, AM I TO GET ANY CONFIRMATIONS AT ALL TODAY?
WE ARE SUPPOSED TO BE INVADING MECHANICSBURG!
WE'RE TRYING, MA'AM! BUT EVERYTHING'S GONE ALL HIGGLEDY-PIGGLEDY!
...BELIEVE IT OR NOT, LIEUTENANT, I RATHER PRIDE MYSELF ON HOW WELL WE FACILITATE COMMUNICATION.
YOU SHOULD TRY IT.
WHAT WAS THAT?
PLEASE REPEAT.
ALL THE UNITS WE'RE SUPPOSED TO BE COORDINATING—
WE'RE... WE'RE LOSING THEM!
WHAT?!
RUMBLETOYS?
NO ANSWER!
NINTH AETHERIC?
NO ANSWER!
KNIFEGRINDERS?
NO ANSWER!
WIND WALKERS?
THEY CUT OFF!
DOCKING BAY SIX—WHAT IS THE STATUS OF INCOMING ACCURSED DRAGON?
BAY SIX? BAY SIX—PLEASE RESPOND...
THE HELL IS GOING ON?!
WE'LL MISS THE FIGHTING!
WRONG!

JÄGERS! HOW DARE YOU BETRAY—!
HYU IZ CONFUZED, SVEETHOT—
DE HETERODYNE IZ DE VUN WE AIN'T BETRAYINK TODAY!
DE BARON KNOWS DOT.
THAT...THAT GIRL IS A FAKE!
HYU SURE 'BOUT DOT?
YES!
NIZE HATS, LADIES.
AND DON'T HURT MY PEOPLE! WE'RE NON-COMBATANTS!
HO, YEZ? IZ DOT VOT HYU CALLS FLYINK AROUND MELTING PIPPLE DOWN BELOW INTO LEEDLE PUDDLES?
NONSENSE! WE ARE A COMMUNICATIONS—
pft. UND HY IZ DE PRINCESS HASENPFEFFER OV SPÄTZLE.
DE REST OV DE FLEET IS SECURE, JORGI!
GOOT. GOOT.
CRUNCH!
HOKAY, KEEDS, HYU KIN LAND DIS TING—
HMM—HOWZ ABOUT RIGHT OUTSIDE DER MONSTERS' GATE?
VE GOTS TO BE READY TO MARCH IN, YAH?
BUT...YOU CAN'T GO INTO TOWN, CAN YOU?
DOT'S RIGHT, DOLLINK, NOT YET—
BUT SOON!
AAAAAAAH!
AAAAAAAH!
HO-HO! VERRA SOON!
LIKE RIGHT NOW!

THE STREETS OF MECHANICSBURG—
SIR!
WHAT IS IT, SPINOZA?
GOT A SITUATION, SIR!
ANOTHER ONE?!
WE'VE FINALLY TAKEN SOME PRISONERS.
THEY'RE JUST TOWNSPEOPLE, BUT THEY WERE REALLY GIVING US A HARD TIME.
HOW MANY?
ABOUT EIGHT.
ANYBODY IMPORTANT? DOCTORS OR CITY COUNCIL?
UM, NO, SIR. I THINK THEY'RE BAKERS.
OKAY. SHOOT 'EM.
SHOOT—BUT WE CAN'T DO THAT!
DON'T TELL ME YOU'RE OUT OF BULLETS?
THEY'RE JUST A BUNCH OF OLD MEN! CIVILIANS!
WHO DO YOU THINK IS FIGHTING US?!
"CIVILIANS" HAVE WIPED OUT HALF OUR SQUAD!
I'VE NEVER SEEN RESISTANCE LIKE THIS!
THEY'RE SHOPKEEPERS FOR ARES' SAKE!
THEY DON'T CARE WHO'S IN CHARGE! THEY'LL CHEAT ANYBODY!
WELL, THIS IS MECHANICSBURG, SIR.
THEY'RE NOT HAPPY UNLESS A HETERODYNE IS IN CHARGE.
WELL THEN, THEIR HETERODYNE CAN PROTECT THEM.

DON'T LOOK AT *ME* WHEN YOU'RE COVERING PRISONERS!
SIR! SORRY, SIR!
TREAT THEM WITH *RESPECT!*
YES, SIR!
NOW, SHOOT 'EM!
YE— *WHAT?!*
ATTENTION!
FORM A FIRING LINE!
READY—
AIM—
DOOOM
THE *DOOM BELL!*
THAT GIRL! SHE *IS* THE HETERODYNE!
WHAT SHOULD WE DO WITH *THESE* GUYS?
TIE 'EM UP. THEY'RE JUST KIDS.
AND THE ONE GIVING THE *ORDERS?*
OH, *HIM* WE TREAT WITH *RESPECT!*

MAMA GKIKA'S
STOP! WE'RE HERE.
UM, GIL? NO, WE'RE NOT.
THIS ISN'T CASTLE WULFENBACH, IT'S A BEER HALL.
IT'S NOT JUST A BEER HALL.
BUT THERE AREN'T ANY WULFENBACH TROOPS HERE—
I'M NOT SO SURE ABOUT THAT—
BUT A BEER HALL?
IT'S NOT JUST A BEER HALL.
LOOK, I CAN SEE THAT THEO IS IN PAIN.
THESE CATS AREN'T THE SMOOTHEST RIDES.
IT'S JUST MY ARM!
I WON'T HOLD YOU BACK!
NO, YOU WON'T. BECAUSE YOU'LL BE HERE.
IN A BEER HALL.
IT'S NOT JUST A BEER HALL!
SORRY, SVEETHOT, VE'S CLOSED—
OOOH! IT'S YOU! AGAIN! COME ON IN!
IT'D BETTER BE JUST A BEER HALL!
OOOH, IS SOMEONE FEELING SHY?
WILL YOU PLEASE TELL MAMMA I'M HERE?!

SO— THEY'RE JÄGERS...? I THINK?
NO, THOSE ARE COSTUMES... SORT OF...
BUT WHY—?
—SO AGATHA SHOULD BE DONE ANY TIME NOW.
DOT'S GOOT, 'CAUSE HY GOTS A HALL FULL OV EEDIOTS WHO'S CHUST ABOUT READY TO BURST.
COFFEE?
HEE! HYU VANNA FIND OUT, CUTIE PIE?
NO, I, I DON'T THINK I DO...
THANKS. SO, CAN I LEAVE THESE TWO HERE, UNTIL THE FIGHTING'S OVER?
OV CAUZE! VE GET HEEM FIXED OP TOOT SVEETY!
DOT'S FRENCH!
I LIKE MY COFFEE LIKE I LIKE MY WOMEN MEAN!
...RIGHT. I'LL BE OFF, THEN.
THANKS FOR THE UM—
COFFEE?
OH, DER'S NO BOGZ DIS TIME. HONEST.
AH—VAIT. VUN MORE THING—
MAMA GKIKA'S MECHANICS BAR
HYU POPPA, HE PROTECTED MY BOYZ.
HY VILL NOT FORGET DOT.
AH. AND THE JÄGERS SERVED US LOYALLY.
MEMORY GOES BOTH WAYS, MADAM.
...AND WE'LL BE DEFENDING THE TOWN TOGETHER SOON ENOUGH—
ASSUMING I CAN TAKE CONTROL OF MY FATHER'S FORCES QUICKLY.
ASK FOR CREDIT
NOW, I MUST—

YEZ! DE BELL IZ *RINGING!*
VE HAS A HETERODYNE AGAIN!
tsk. KEEDS TODAY.
KENT EVEN TAKE A LEEDLE *EXISTENTIAL DESPAIR*.
HO VELL. S'POZE HY GOTTA—
AGATHA!
SHE *DID IT!*
SAY—IZ HYU OKEH?
DE SOUND OV DE DOOM BELL—
IT MEANS SHE'S TAKEN THE CASTLE!
SHE'S ALIVE AND FIGHTING!
IT SOUNDS *BEAUTIFUL!*
HOKAY! HY'S GUN GO GET MY BOYZ!
DE LADY HETERODYNE'S CONSORT NEEDS AN *ESCORT!*

WELCOME HOME, LADY HETERODYNE.

THANK YOU, HERR VON MEKKHAN,
BUT I CAN'T HELP BUT NOTICE THAT MY HOME APPEARS TO BE ON *FIRE*.
AH. NOTICED THAT, HAVE YOU?
AND...WHAT DO YOU THINK ABOUT THAT?
WHAT DO I *THINK* ABOUT IT?
I THINK WE NEED TO GET BUSY AND *CRUSH* EVERYONE WHO'S *ATTACKING US!*
THE TOWN IS BEING *INVADED!*
EXCELLENT!
AN *INVASION* IS EXCELLENT?
OH, IT'S *NOT THAT*.
IT'S THAT YOU *NOTICED*. YOU *CARE!*
THAT'S NOT ALWAYS THE CASE, YOU KNOW!
IT IS AN *ENCOURAGING* SIGN!
WE ALSO LIKE THE *CRUSHING* PART!
THE HETERODYNES HAVE ALWAYS *PROTECTED* MECHANICSBURG—
BUT *SOME* OF YOU ARE *BETTER* AT IT THAN OTHERS.
IN THE YEAR OF THREE WINTERS, YOUR GRANDFATHER SET *THE OLD TOWN HALL* ON FIRE.
HE KEPT IT BURNING FOR FIVE WHOLE MONTHS!
YOUR GREAT-GRANDFATHER DECIDED ALL THE CHILDREN SHOULD BE *MAGNETIZED* SO WE'D NEVER GET *LOST!*
...I USED TO GET STUCK TO THE IRON BRIDGE EVERY TIME MOTHER SENT ME OUT FOR CHEESE.
YOUR GREAT-GRAND UNCLE OMINOX WOULD GOAD ENEMIES INTO *ATTACKING*—
AND THEN YELL *"SURPRISE!"*
OH, I HAD SUCH A CRUSH ON HIM!
...AND HERE I WAS WORRIED THAT I WOULDN'T BE ANY GOOD AT THIS.
HEH. YOU HAVE FIFTY GENERATIONS OF LOWERED EXPECTATIONS WORKING FOR YOU.
TWO MINUTES, AND SHE HASN'T KILLED *ANYONE!*
A *NEW RECORD!*

VERY FUNNY. HO HO.
NOW, WHAT'S OUR SITUATION?
THE CASTLE SAID IT WAS UNDER ATTACK.
IT *IS*.
WULFENBACH AND THOSE CATS TOOK OUT ALL THE ENEMIES AT THIS GATE—
AND, ACCORDING TO THAT PACK OF OLD BANDITS BEHIND ME—
WHO'S OLD, YOU *INSOLENT PUP?!*
THE DOOM BELL WILL HAVE KNOCKED OUT A *LOT* OF THE REST.
Die!
Death to the witch of Mechanicsburg!
Die! Die! Die!
SO IT'S A SAFE BET THAT ANYTHING LEFT IS GOING TO BE *TRICKY*.

...I REALLY HOPE THIS THING STILL HAS ENOUGH POWER...
TWIST
CLIK
HA!
ZAK-AK!
Dieeeeeeeeeeeeeeeeeeeee
ZOW!
AAAH!
STOP...
eee...
RIGHT. I'LL NEED A FULL RUNDOWN OF EVERYTHING I'VE GOT TO WORK WITH.
I WANT THESE FOOLS OUT OF MY TOWN–
WHILE THERE STILL IS A TOWN!

TIME TO DIE!
OH, NO YOU DON'T-
fizzle
CLIK CLIK
TIME TO GO!
PAF! PAF! PAF!
SCIENCE HAS FAILED ME.

FALSE HETERODYNE! ACKNOWLEDGE ME AS YOUR MASTER-
AND I WILL LET YOU POLISH MY BEAUTIFUL CLAW!
UM, SO, ABOUT THOSE DEFENSES—?

THE EMPIRE DISABLED OUR *OBVIOUS* WEAPONS—BUT WE'RE WORKING ON THEM.
WE HAVE SAPPERS IN THE TUNNELS AND, OF COURSE, THE TUNNELS THEMSELVES,
VARIOUS TRADESMEN WHO USE DANGEROUS TOOLS ON A DAILY BASIS,

REVEAL WHERE YOU HAVE HIDDEN THE STORM KING-
OR BE REDUCED TO A PITIFUL TWO DIMENSIONS!
HAUS OF WAFFLES
EAT!
NOT JUST FOR BREAKFAST
MENU
AND THE TOWN MILITIA, BUT THEY'VE MOSTLY JUST GOT SMALL ARMS AND WHISTLES.

WHISTLES?!
REALLY *LOUD* WHISTLES.
OH, AND FRAU HOOGLE'S GOT A *REALLY* MEAN DOG...
THAT'S *IT?!*
CENTURIES OF MAD SCIENCE AND WE HAVE

AH—LADY HETERODYNE. MY MASTER DEMANDS YOUR HAND IN MARRIAGE AT YOUR EARLIEST CONVENIENCE.
I DIDN'T SAY *THAT*. WE *HAVE* STUFF—
BUT WITHOUT THE *CASTLE*, I DON'T KNOW IF IT'LL *WORK*.

RHAAAAAAR!
OH, I SAY!
UNTIL WE KNOW, WE'LL JUST HAVE TO RELY ON

GRHAA!
AIEEEEE!
WOW. MONSTERS, HUH?
OH, YES.
AH. HERR VON MEKKHAN!
SNOZ CAN BE OUT. THEY RANG THE BELL. THEY DID!
THE FITTING ROOM
CORSETS BUSTLES and DISTINCTIVE OUTFITS of QUALITY
INDEED THEY DID!
LADY HETERODYNE, THIS IS SNOZ.
SNOZ, THIS IS THE NEW HETERODYNE.
HELLO.
A... GIRL?
YES.
huh. SNOZ NEVER SEEN A GIRL HETERODYNE BEFORE.
AND...?
...AND NEW HETERODYNE CUTE!
SNOZ LIKE!
...BUT SNOZ ALREADY IN COMMITTED RELATIONSHIP.
I...I'LL KEEP THAT IN MIND.
SNOZ MUST GO SMASH THINGS NOW!
...HOW MANY MONSTERS?
HMMM... WELL, I'D SAY NOT TOO MANY RIGHT NOW...
BOOM! BOOM! BOOM!
HALLOOOOOO!
AAH—!
—BUT IT SOUNDS LIKE THERE ARE A WHOLE LOT MORE ON THEIR WAY.

MECHANICSBURG'S EASTERN GATE—
HALLOOOOOO!
Poppa— what *is* that?
I...I DON'T...
IT'S THE *JÄGERS!* THEY'RE COMING *HOME!*
BOOM!
BA- DOOM
DOOM DOOM!
BOOM!
—THE JÄGERHALL! THE BUTCHERS' GUILD HAS BEEN USING IT AS A *SLAUGHTERHOUSE!*
I *TOLD* YOU IT WON'T BE A *PROBLEM,* ITZOKK.
GUNNERY POST XI
YEAH. WE WON'T EVEN HAVE TO *REDECORATE.*
HALLOOOOOOOO!
REAL JÄGERMONSTERS?
BUT...I THOUGHT THERE WOULD BE *MORE* OF THEM?
WELL, IT *HAS* BEEN A *LONG TIME*...
AND WHAT'S SO *FUNNY,* GRAMPS?
HEH HEH! YOU ARE!

THESE ARE THE *JÄGERS* WE'RE TALKING ABOUT!

RIGHT NOW OUR *ENEMIES* ARE WATCHING THEM ADVANCE, AND THINKING THE SAME THING YOU ARE—

BUT DON'T *YOU* BE THAT DUMB.

RIGHT BOYS?

DOT'S RIGHT!

HYU LEESEN TO HYU GRAN'POPPA, KEEDS!

VE IZ BEINK SO—TELL UND SNEAKY-LIKE!

YAH! DOT'S SY-KO-LOGICAL WARFARE, DOT IZ!

VAT *IZ* DEY TEACHINK IN SKOOL DESE DAYZ?

BAH! SISSY SCHTUFF! POISON! COUNTERFITTINK! POLITICKS!

HOY! VE COME BACK JUST IN TIME!

HELLO, LEETLE GURL! LATER HY VILL SHOW HYU HOW TO THROW A KNIFE!

OOH... *REALLY?*

HELLO, MITKO! NIZE LOOKINK KEEDS!

THANK YOU, BORISLAV, WELCOME HOME!

TENK HYU! HOKAY BOYS, READY TO FIGHT!

YEZ!
SALE ON SHOES!
MECHANICSBURG MONSTER AND CONSTRUCT CREDIT UNION
JOBS
BY MONSTERS FOR MONSTERS
CREDIT GOOD!
VOO HOO! TIME TO PAINT DE TOWN *RED!*
WELCOME
VLAD'S VEGETABLES

CASTLE WULFENBACH—

ALL THE JAGERS ARE THERE, SIR!

IT'S *IMPOSSIBLE*— UNLESS THEY SOMEHOW KNEW ABOUT ALL THIS *DAYS AGO!*

OH, I'M *SURE* THEY *DID.*

STOP!

INTRUDER!

SOK

I AM NO *INTRUDER!*

OTHAR TRYGGVASSEN

GENTLEMAN ADVENTURER—

WAS *INVITED!*

TRYGG— *AH!* YOU MEAN,

YOU *FOUND* HIM?!

BUT OF COURSE! ALLOW ME TO PRESENT:
fwop
GILGAMESH WULFENBACH—

MASTER OF DISGUISE!

IN CASTLE HETERODYNE—
SWEET LIGHTNING!
WHAT ON EARTH WAS THAT?!
WHY, THAT MUST HAVE BEEN THE DOOM BELL!
ASTONISHING!
BUT-YOU-GETWIN-
WERE YOU UNAFFECTED?
OH, YES. DEAD, YOU KNOW.
BUT I AM WORRIED ABOUT MY FRAULEIN SNAUG.
COME ON, UP UP!
STRENGTH OF THE SPIDER, AND ALL!
SO SHE REALLY IS THE HETERODYNE.
WELL SPOTTED, TIKTOFFEN.
I WONDER IF ANY OF HIS PLANS CAME THROUGH.
MY DEAR FELLOW. HE'S SO CONVOLUTED, HOW WOULD HE KNOW?
HA!
OH. LOOK.
IT'S LITTLE WILHELM!
I DO HOPE SHE'S ALIVE-
THEY'RE NO FUN WHEN THEY'RE DEAD.
I SAY, SIR.
OH, PRESENT COMPANY EXCEPTED, OF COURSE.
OH, GOOD. SHE'S ALIVE AFTER ALL.
clink
AH! HER COLLAR!
YOUR-MY COLLAR!
RATTLE
THE CASTLE-
IT'S REPAIRED!
THEY RANG THE DOOM BELL!
WE'RE FREE!

THE TOWER OF THE DOOM BELL—
gnnurggh...
HEH HEH HEH. YOU ARE STILL ALIVE, LITTLE ADVENTURER?
EXTRAORDINARY.
hnrrrg...
YOU WANTED THE TREASURE OF THE HETERODYNES, YES?
WELL, I DON'T KNOW IF YOU CARE ANY MORE-
BUT IT'S HERE.
pft.
YOU WOKE ME UP FOR THIS?
nnnhik...

A HETERODYNE HAS RETURNED TO US.
TIME TO DO YOUR JOB, OLD FELLOW.
HEY-LOOK AT THE TOWN! I THINK WE'RE BEING ATTACKED!
...YOU'RE NOT REALLY A MORNING PERSON, ARE YOU?
HOLD ON-HOLD ON-THIS MEANS I GET TO DO THIS THE FUN WAY!
BUT WHAT'S THIS? YOU GOT ME BREAKFAST?
I'D PREFER A CROISSANT...
I'M AFRAID NOT. TECHNICALLY, THIS PERSON HAS AIDED US.
hrmgg...
"TECHNICALLY," EH?
(SIGH) FINE.
LONG LIVE THE NEW HETERODYNE! REJOICE, YOU!
CLINK!
vglmbp?
TINK!
TSK. THAT WAS UNSATISFYING. SO ANYWAY, WHAT ABOUT YOUR JOB?
DOESN'T LOOK LIKE YOU'RE DOING MUCH DOWN THERE.
I AM REPAIRED, BUT MY POWER IS NEARLY DEPLETED.
I AM DOING WHAT I CAN-
...gold?
AND OTHERS ARE COMING.
HM. WILL THEY BE ENOUGH?
THAT WILL DEPEND ON THE HETERODYNE.
gold...dragon? the...the guardian is real...the legend is...is TRUE!
EVERYTHING DEPENDS ON HER, NOW.
OH, I SEE-BECAUSE THE REST OF US ARE CHOPPED LIVER.
YOU MIGHT AS WELL BE, AS LONG AS YOU JUST STAND AROUND HERE TALKING.
OKAY, I'M GOING, I'M GOING.
I'VE WON!

THE STREETS OF MECHANICSBURG—
OKAY. I THINK WE'VE LOST THEM.
GOOD! I DIDN'T KNOW THEY EVEN MADE THOSE ELECTRIC WASPS ANY MORE.
THEY DON'T. YOU CAN'T GET THE PARTS.
REALLY? WE SHOULD SELL THOSE...
INVASION SALE
ALL RIGHT, WELL, FIRST OF ALL, I NEED TO GET TO THE TOP OF THE CITY WALLS.
NO WAY! I'M TAKING YOU TO THE CATHEDRAL, WHERE IT'S SAFE!
WHAT?! HOW AM I SUPPOSED TO GET ANYTHING DONE FROM THERE?!
YOU WON'T. THE JÄGERS AND THE OTHER MONSTERS—
THEY'LL DO THE FIGHTING.
BUT—
YOU'RE THE LAST HETERODYNE—
YOU HAVE TO BE KEPT SAFE UNTIL THE TOWN IS SECURE.
YOU'VE DONE YOUR PART!
YOU FIXED THE CASTLE!
THE DOOM BELL RANG!
AT THIS POINT, WHAT ELSE CAN YOU DO?
WRONG QUESTION.
I AM THE HETERODYNE.
MY TOWN IS UNDER ATTACK.
THE QUESTION IS:
WHAT CAN'T I DO?

HO! NOW DOT'S DE RIGHT ATTITUDE, SVEETHOT!
BUT EVEN IF HYU IZ A KREZY STRONG SPARK—
IT NEVER HURTZ TO HAVE A NIZE ARMY TO BACK HYU UP!
HETERODYNE TONIC! YUM!
SALE NOX OF PARIS
DOLLINK

ZO, HYU IZ DE NEW HETERODYNE!
VELCOME HOME, SVEETIE!
SQUEEZE!
ERK! AH...
UM... WHO ARE YOU?
HO! JÄGER GENERAL GKIKA AT HYU SERVICE, M'LADY!
THANK YOU. I...I DIDN'T REALIZE THERE WERE OTHER GENERALS.
HO! HYU JUST MET DOSE THREE OLD OGRES ON CASTLE WULFENBACH, YEZ?
IZ A GOOD THING DERE'S MORE OF US DEN DOT.
DUN VORRY. VEN DIS IZ ALL CALMED DOWN, VE'LL MAKE SURE HYU MEET ALL OF US.
...IN THE SAME ROOM? AT THE SAME TIME?
DUN VORRY. JUST BRING A BIG STICK.
BUT VE GOTS NO TIME FOR DE TALKING.
MY BOYZ TELL ME DERE'S MORE TROUBLE ON DE VAY—
UND HY HAVEN'T SEEN ANY DECENT TROUBLE IN AGES.
DIS IZ GONNA BE FUN.
GRARRR!

SOON—
ta-dah! DE HETERODYNE'S OBSERVATION TOWER!
DE PERFECT PLACE TO DIRECT BATTLES UND SPIT ON PIPPLE!
UND VEN HYU IZ NOT FIGHTING, HYU CAN BRING HYU BOYFRIEND UP HERE!
HEH. DIS PLACE GETS HIT BY LIGHTNING ALL DE TIME—IZ VERRA ROMANTIC!
(sigh.) YOU SAY THERE'S "TROUBLE" COMING.
WHAT KIND?
VUN BIG ARMY COMING UP DE PASS FROM STURMHALTEN. LOTSA NASTY MONSTERS.
UND VOT LOOKS LIKE EFFRYTING DE BARON'S GOT— HEADING IN AT US FROM ALL SIDES.
MONSTERS... COMING FROM STURMHALTEN?
WHAT ABOUT THE ATTACKERS STILL IN MECHANICSBURG?
THE DOOM BELL SHUT MOST OF THEM DOWN.
AS LONG AS WE CAN KEEP ANY NEW ENEMIES FROM GETTING INSIDE THE WALLS—
WE SHOULD HAVE THE ONES ALREADY HERE MOPPED UP PRETTY QUICKLY.
SMASH!
HEY!
I SAID REJOICE!

I HAVE TO ADMIT, I HAD HOPED FOR MORE HELP FROM THE CASTLE—
I'VE MADE ALL THE REPAIRS IT ASKED FOR,
BUT IT ISN'T GENERATING ANY NEW POWER.
IT'S BEEN RUNNING ON STORED ENERGY FOR YEARS—
AND THAT'S MOSTLY BEEN DRAINED.
AT THIS POINT, I DON'T KNOW IF IT EVEN...
YES! IT WAS A CLOSE CALL!
I NEARLY WENT TO SLEEP RIGHT IN THE MIDDLE OF THIS LOVELY BATTLE!
AH! THE CASTLE!
WELL! YOU'RE SOUNDING MUCH BETTER!
YOUR CHIEF MINION HAS RESTORED MY MAIN GENERATOR!
VELL, DOT'S GOOT!
—THAT'S WONDERFUL!
BUT I AM STILL WEAK... IT WILL TAKE TIME TO BUILD UP A SUFFICIENT CHARGE TO DO ANYTHING IMPORTANT.
OH? HOW LONG?
HMM. ALL NON-ESSENTIAL SYSTEMS ARE ALREADY SHUT DOWN-
WITH EVERYTHING SHUNTED TO OFFENSE-
I WOULD SAY, ABOUT THREE YEARS.
THREE YEARS.
GIVE OR TAKE A FEW WEEKS, YES.
I SEE.
LESS THAN IDEAL, I KNOW...
...WHAT OTHER MONSTERS DO WE HAVE?
WELL, IF WE CAN GET ALL OUR ENEMIES TO A PICNIC ON TINY MONSTER ISLAND...
BUT THREE YEARS FROM NOW...
WATCH OUT!

...SO, WE'VE GOT TEAMS WORKING ON THE BIGGER DEFENSES—

AND THE *CASTLE'S* GOT US GOING ALL OUT ON A BUNCH OF MYSTERIOUS REPAIRS OF ITS *OWN.*

IT'S BEING REALLY CAGEY ABOUT THEM, BUT IT *INSISTS* THEY'LL *HELP*...

HEE HEE. YOU'LL BE *SO SURPRISED*...

WELL, ASSUMING YOU'RE STILL *ALIVE,* OF COURSE...

ARGH. THIS IS *TERRIBLE.*

WELL, AT LEAST IT'S NOT JUST *US*—

OUR *ENEMIES* ARE *ALSO* RUNNING AROUND LIKE HEADLESS CONSTRUCTS.

WE'RE *UNBELIEVABLY LUCKY.*

—BUT I HAVE TO SAY I'M *SURPRISED*. BEING UNDER THE PROTECTION OF THE EMPIRE IS *NO EXCUSE!*

EVEN WITH THE CASTLE DOWN—TO LET THE *MAJOR DEFENSES* FALL INTO SUCH *DISREPAIR*—

pfu. DOT VASN'T *OUR FAULT*.

DE BARON *DISARMED* ALL DE REALLY *GOOT SCHTUFF*.

WHAT? *WHY?!*

TO KEEP DE REST OV DER EMPIRE *HAPPY*.

"KLAUS VOS FRIENDS MIT BILL AND BARRY, BUT *HISTORICALLY*, DE VULFENBACHS AND THE HETERODYNES VERE *ENEMIES.*"

RODYNE MUSE

THIS MONTH:
500 YEARS
of CRUSHING
-machines!
-monsters!
-philosophy!
Y KIDS!
SEE THE
RUSHING
ZOO!

"DER HETERODYNES VAS ENEMIES VIT *EFFRYBODY!*"

"EFFRYVUN IN EUROPA FELT BETTER VIT MECHANICSBURG DISARMED."

"VELL, EVERYVUN BUT *US,* OV CAUZE."

HETERODYNE
MUSEUM
AND
CRUS
CLOSED
ZOO
COME FOR THE CRUSHING
STAY FOR THE SNOW CONES

"WE'D TRY TO QUIETLY MAKE REPAIRS WHERE THEY WOULDN'T SHOW."
"BUT THE BARON WOULD ALWAYS SEND SOMEONE TO DISARM THINGS AGAIN."
"THEN WE'D SNEAK BACK AND FIX THINGS SO THE MACHINES WOULD ONLY LOOK BROKEN."
"AND THE BARON'S PEOPLE WOULD COME BACK AND BREAK THINGS AGAIN, IN NEW WAYS."
"THIS WENT ON FOR YEARS."
HALL OF DEATH-DEALING ELECTRO-MECHANICAL FUN!
WHY DIDN'T HE JUST TAKE IT ALL AWAY?
WELL, HE DID TAKE SOME OF IT—
BUT FRANKLY, IT WOULD BE HARD TO MOVE EVERYTHING,
AND MOST OF IT'S FINE WHERE IT IS, AS LONG AS IT DOESN'T WORK.
KONK!
LUCKY FOR US, WE'VE BECOME VERY GOOD AT REPAIRING THINGS.
DEFENSES CONTROLLED BY THE CASTLE MAY NOT HELP US MUCH RIGHT NOW,
BUT THERE ARE LOTS OF OTHER THINGS WE CAN USE ONCE WE GET THEM RUNNING.
THE SCREAMERS SHOULD BE BACK WITHIN THE HOUR—
BUT THE LAVA CANNONS WILL TAKE AT LEAST ANOTHER TWO DAYS.
HM. HOW QUICKLY DO YOU THINK WE CAN GET GIL'S LIGHTNING GENERATORS ANALYZED AND REPLACED?
YOU KNOW, THOSE THINGS HE HAD ALL ALONG THE CITY WALLS?
I KNOW SOME OF THEM MELTED, BUT—
LADY HETERODYNE, PLEASE.
WE'VE HAD PEOPLE WORKING ON THAT SINCE HE FIRST SET THEM UP.
THOSE THINGS WERE AMAZING!
OH, I KNEW THERE WAS A REASON I LIKED THIS PLACE!

CASTLE WULFENBACH—

AH, **NO.** I DON'T ***THINK*** SO.

FOOM!
OH! S-SORRY, SIR!

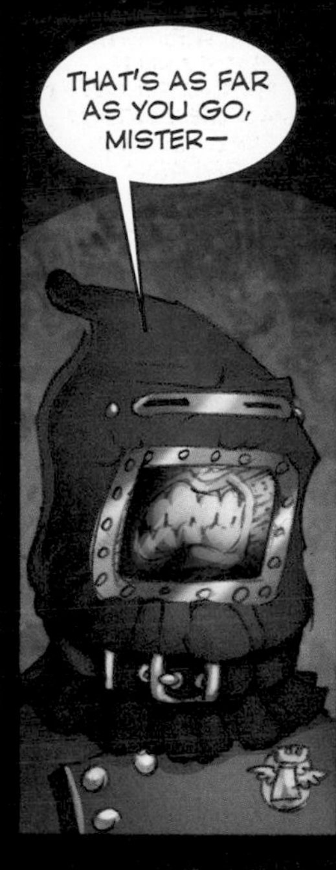

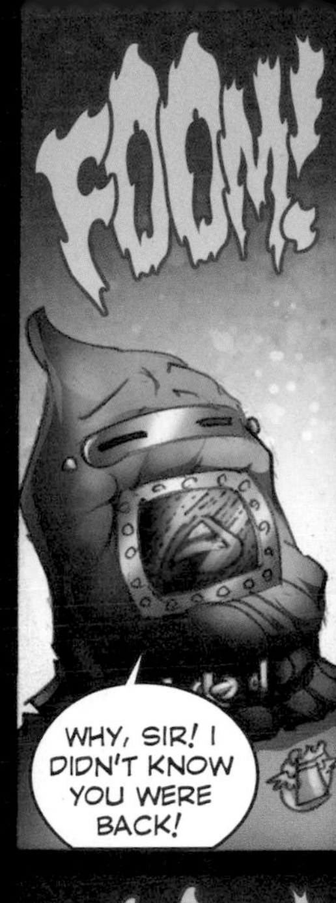

THAT'S AS FAR AS YOU GO, MISTER—

FOOM!
WHY, SIR! I DIDN'T KNOW YOU WERE BACK!

YOU ARE NOT AUTHORIZED...

AUTHORIZATION ACCEPTED.

GUARDS! WE'VE GOT AN INTRUDER ON THE—

FOOM!
OOOOOOH. IT ***IS*** YOU!

OH, COME ON. YOU EXPECT ME TO BELIEVE YOU—
JUST BECAUSE OF THAT ***RIDICULOUS***—
PUNCH!
WHEN THIS IS ALL SETTLED, ***YOU*** GET A ***PROMOTION.***

ARE YOU ***SURE*** IT'S ***HIM?***
YES! I MEAN, WE WEREN'T AT ***FIRST***—
BUT HE'S GOT THE MOST ***AMAZING***—

YES. IT'S ***REALLY ME.***
YES, I'M ***REALLY BACK.***
I AM NOT A ***SPY***-
I AM NOT AN ***IMPOSTER***-
AND I AM ***NOT AMUSED!***
GILGEMESH WULFENBACH
SCHMOTT GUY!

GILGAMESH WULFENBACH
SCHMOTT GUY!
BORIS!
ER, YES, MASTER GILGAMESH?
YES! THAT'S ME!
OF COURSE IT'S ME!
WHO ELSE COULD EVER WEAR SO MAJESTIC AND COMMANDING A HAT?
UM, SURELY NO ONE, SIR.
OH, GOOD. SO WE ARE ALL AGREED THAT I AM, IN FACT, ME?
WELL, YES! OF COURSE!
GOOD!
YOU!
eep!
TAKE THIS.
HIDE IT IN A SAFE PLACE-
AND NEVER SPEAK OF IT AGAIN.
YES SIR!
whew.
I HEARD THERE WAS A HAT!
...YOU'RE DELUSIONAL.

AND I WANT AN EXPLANATION, DUPREE.
WEREN'T YOU WITH MY FATHER? WHAT HAPPENED?
HE SENT ME OUT OF THE HOSPITAL!
—AND YOU WENT?!
WELL, YES!
BECAUSE DOING WHAT HE SAYS IS MY JOB!
OH, AND YOU ALWAYS FOLLOW ORDERS.
HEY! I FOLLOWED HIS ORDERS! EVEN WHEN I THOUGHT THEY WERE STUPID!
HE SAYS GO DO THIS STUPID THING—I GO DO IT!
AND WHEN THE ATTACK CAME, I HAD TO RUN ALL THE WAY BACK TO THE HOSPITAL!
BUT I COULDN'T...I COULDN'T FIND HIM!
I COULDN'T FIND HIM ANYWHERE!
AND... AND...
AND THEN THE WHOLE PLACE CAME DOWN, AND I COULDN'T SAVE HIM!
SOB SOB
I REALLY, REALLY TRIED!
I...I KNOW.
...AND IF YOU COULDN'T DO IT—NO ONE COULD.
snif. YOU HAVE MADE ME CRY.
FOR THIS I WILL KILL YOU.
YES, YES.
EVERYONE IS WAITING...
HERR BARON.

OH.
OH, *NO*.
THIS DOESN'T FEEL RIGHT.
WELL, I SHOULD *HOPE NOT!*
START LIKING IT TOO MUCH, AND I'LL STICK AN *KNIFE* IN YOUR—
NOT *THAT*. BORIS—
CALLING ME "BARON"—
SURELY YOU HAVE MORE FAITH IN MY FATHER THAN *THAT*.
HAVE...HAVE THEY FOUND HIS *BODY?*
NO, SIR. BUT I AM ACTING ON HIS *DIRECT ORDERS*.
WHAT?
YOUR FATHER GAVE ME VERY CLEAR INSTRUCTIONS REGARDING THE ACTION I AM TO TAKE IF THERE IS EVER CAUSE TO BELIEVE HIM DEAD.
I AM TO PUBLICLY RECOGNIZE *YOU* AS THE NEW BARON *WITHOUT DELAY*.
I BELIEVE HIS INTENTION WAS TO ENSURE AN ORDERLY TRANSITION AND PRESERVE THE PEACE THROUGHOUT THE EMPIRE.
I SEE.
WELL, YES...
BUT I WILL NOT ASSUME HIS *TITLE*.
THAT SHOULD BE NO TROUBLE. IN THAT CASE, YOUR FATHER LEFT ORDERS TO USE ONE OF *YOURS*—
YOUR HIGHNESS.
OH, FOR...I CAN'T EVEN IMAGINE WHAT *THAT'S* ABOUT.
JUST ONE MORE THING HE COULDN'T BE BOTHERED TO *TELL* ME, I SUPPOSE...
...*WOW*.
WHAT?
I *ALWAYS WONDERED* HOW HE PLANNED TO RUN OFF AND LEAVE *YOU* HOLDING THE BAG.
IMPRESSIVE.

ENOUGH.
ALIVE OR DEAD, MY FATHER ISN'T HERE—
AND WE NEED TO ACT QUICKLY.
WHAT'S OUR CURRENT SITUATION?
WELL, WE'D BEEN KEEPING WELL BACK, CONCENTRATING ON SECURING EVERYTHING FOR FIFTY KILOMETERS AROUND THE TOWN—
"ONCE THE SITUATION BECAME REALLY BAD, WE SENT FOR REINFORCEMENTS.
WE'VE BEEN BRINGING IN MORE AND MORE UNITS AS QUICKLY AS WE CAN.
THEY'VE BEEN ARRIVING FOR DAYS, BUT WE'VE HAD A LOT OF FORCES OUT ON THE BORDERS LATELY, AND THOSE WILL HAVE A LONG WAY TO TRAVEL."
MOST OF THE WORST ATTACKERS HAVE BEEN PUT DOWN, BUT NOW THERE'S A HORDE OF MONSTERS COMING UP FROM STURMHALTEN.
WE'VE LOST CONTACT WITH OUR PEOPLE THERE, AND EVERYONE WE'VE SENT HAS BEEN KILLED OR—
...OR?
OR HAS APPARENTLY JOINED THEM.
AH. THE "OTHER"—
WHAT? HOW?!
ISN'T THE LADY HETERODYNE THE OTHER?
YOUR FATHER—
NO.
WELL, SHE'S ONE OF THEM—A LITTLE—BUT ONLY SOMETIMES.
...WE'RE WORKING ON IT, OKAY?
AM I THE ONLY PERSON WHO WORRIES ABOUT THIS?!
I'M WORRIED.
WELL, THAT'S—
I'M WORRIED I WON'T GET A CHANCE TO SHOOT HER.
NO SHOOTING!

FIRST OF ALL, SPREAD THE WORD TO THE TROOPS—ALL ATTACKS ON MECHANICSBURG ARE TO *CEASE IMMEDIATELY.*
AH. ALREADY DONE, SIR.
ALREADY? BUT, WHY—
BECAUSE *I TOLD* THEM TO.
WE'RE NOW CONCENTRATING ON DEFENDING THE TOWN AND RESTORING THE PEACE.
WHAT ARE *YOU* DOING *HERE?!*
RUNNING *YOUR*
WHAT *TOOK* YOU SO LONG? WHERE HAVE YOU *BEEN?!*

YOU'RE SUPPOSED TO BE WITH AGATHA!
BORIS, HE'S SUPPOSED TO BE WITH AGATHA!
WHY IS HE HERE?
I KNOW IT'S UNUSUAL, SIR, BUT YOUR FATHER SENT OTHAR TRYGGVASSEN TO GET YOU,
AND HE BROUGHT BACK THIS FELLOW INSTEAD.
WE WERE HAULING THEM BOTH OFF TO THE BRIG—
"AND HE GLANCED—GLANCED—AT THE OPERATIONS TABLE AS HE WAS BEING DRAGGED PAST."
34
"FROM THAT ALONE, HE WAS ABLE TO DEDUCE THAT THE 207TH CHEMICAL HAD BEEN SUBVERTED.
IF THEY'D GONE ANOTHER KILOMETER, THEY WOULD HAVE DESTROYED OUR ENTIRE SUPPLY CHAIN AS WELL AS THE AMMUNITION HAULERS. WITHIN AN HOUR, MOST OF OUR UNITS WOULD HAVE BEEN DEFENSELESS.
"IT WAS HIS IDEA TO CONTAIN THEM WITH THE 43RD AIR AND THE SLOW MOVERS."
HE'S BEEN COORDINATING THE MILITARY EVER SINCE.
hmf. WHO HAS BEEN ASSESSING HIS DECISIONS?
MYSELF, THE DEEP THINKERS, AND THE REST OF THE HIGH COMMAND.
HE'S ACTUALLY MADE SEVERAL MOVES THAT WILL HAVE GREAT LONG-TERM BENEFITS FOR THE EMPIRE...
OH, REALLY.
YES, REALLY! YOU THINK I'M GOING TO MESS AROUND WITH STUPID PLOTTING WHEN AGATHA'S IN DANGER?
HMM. MAYBE...YOU ARE KIND OF STUPID...
—AND ANYWAY, THEY'VE HAD SOMETHING LIKE TWENTY DIFFERENT WEAPONS TRAINED ON ME THE WHOLE TIME!
TWENTY-THREE. BUT I'M IMPRESSED THAT YOU NOTICED.

ALL RIGHT, THEN. SHOW ME WHAT YOU'VE DONE.
GOOD. I'LL SKIP THE OBVIOUS STUFF.
WAIT—YOU'VE DIVERTED THE DROPWALL ENGINES WE WERE SENDING TO BALAN'S GAP.
(sigh) SO MUCH FOR OBVIOUS.
THOSE WERE TO CONTAIN—
CONTAIN WHAT? THERE'S ALREADY AN ARMY ON THE WAY.
AH. SO I SEE. SO WE'LL WANT THE DROPWALLS AS DEFENSIVE UNITS. GOOD.
WELL, BUT THEYRE ONLY GOOD AGAINST GROUND FORCES.
BUT THE EMPIRE STILL CONTROLS THE AIR.
PERHAPS. I'M WORRIED ABOUT THIS FLEET OF SKY—SHARKS. THEY'RE NOT FLYING IN A WULFENBACH PATTERN.
...WELL SPOTTED. THEIR OFFICERS ARE LOYAL TO THE KNIGHTS OF JOVE.
BUT IF YOU DESTROY THE LEADERS OF THE MOGLAR ALLIANCE—
THEY'LL BE IN THIS SHIP HERE—
THEN THE SHARKS, AS WELL AS THE MECHA-SCHNAUZERS AND THE FIFTH WHEEL GUNS, WILL DESPERATELY TRY TO PRETEND THEY WERE NEVER DISLOYAL AT ALL.
BORIS! I WANT THAT SHIP COCOONED AND DROPPED RIGHT NOW.
BUT HANG ON, STURMVORAUS—
DON'T THE KNIGHTS OF JOVE ANSWER TO YOU?
NO.
THEY ANSWERED TO MY FATHER, AND THE HEADS OF THE ORDER.
I WAS PROBABLY WRITTEN OFF AS SOON AS I WAS CAPTURED.
I SERIOUSLY DOUBT MY COMING DOWN WITH SOMETHING AS EXOTIC AS HOGFARB'S RESPLENDENT IMMOLATION WAS AN ACCIDENT.
OH. WELL, TOUGH LUCK ABOUT THE STORM KING THING, THEN.
WULFENBACH.
I HAVE SOME RATHER...UNPLEASANT COUSINS WHO WOULD LOVE TO HAVE ME OUT OF THE LINE OF SUCCESSION.
IF ONE OF THEM BECOMES THE NEW STORM KING—
YOU'RE GOING TO
IT HAD BEEN ME

ON THE WALLS OF MECHANICSBURG—
tsk. HE INSISTS ON USING CONDENSERS.
NO WONDER THESE THINGS MELTED.
GOOT NEWS! DE BONE QVARTER HAZ BEEN CLEARED!
DID YOU NOTICE HE WROTE YOUR NAME ON ALL THE BOLTS?
YEAH. THOSE STREET CLEANING MACHINES YOU REPURPOSED ARE REALLY EFFECTIVE.
OBVIOUSLY HE HAS TOO MUCH TIME ON HIS HANDS.
...BUT I THOUGHT IT WAS VERY SWEET.
...PITY THEY'RE CORRODING THE ACTUAL STREETS...
PICKY, PICKY...WHAT ABOUT THAT GROUP IN THE NORTH WINDINGS?
THE DARK LIGHT GUARDS? THEY'RE PUTTING UP A STRONG RESISTANCE, BUT THEY'RE FALLING BACK TO THE EAST.
PERFECT.
WITH THE DYNE TO THE SOUTH, THEY'LL FUNNEL INTO THE GREENS—
WHERE THEY'LL HAVE NO COVER AT ALL!
NOW, YOU'RE SURE THEY WON'T TAKE THE CATHEDRAL?
OH, I REALLY HOPE THEY TRY.
HOW LONG DO YOU THINK WE'VE GOT BEFORE THE NEXT WAVE OF ATTACKERS ARRIVES?
VELL, DE VULFENBACH FORCES HAFF GOT US PRETTY VELL SURROUNDED RIGHT NOW, VIT MORE SHOWING OP ALL DE TIME—
BUT DEY'S ACTING VEIRD.
HOW CAN YOU— YES?
WE'VE FOUND BÜRGERMEISTER ZUKEN, M'LADY, AND HE WOULD LIKE—
BOOM!

WHAT IS *THAT?!*
THIS END UP
311
IT'S—IT'S A *DROPWALL!*
I'VE SEEN *BLUEPRINTS!*
DE BARON USES DEM TO SURROUND TARGETS!
YEAH, BUT THAT ONE'S FACING THE *WRONG WAY...*
HO. HYU IZ *RIGHT.*
WHOA! THEY'RE DROPPING MORE OF THEM!
A *LOT* MORE!
AH, I GUESS WE SHOULD... GET SOME TROOPS ON THEM.
IT'S *GIL!*
HE *GOT THROUGH!*

WELL, THAT'S A *HUGE* LOAD OFF MY MIND.
WITH GIL BUYING US TIME, WE'LL BE ABLE TO GET A *LOT* MORE DONE ON THE TOWN DEFENSES.
BUT I STILL WANT EVERYONE WORKING AT *TOP SPEED*—
OH, AND CAN *SOMEONE* BRING ME MY *DEATH RAY?*
WELL, WELL. YOU *ARE* A SMART ONE, *AREN'T YOU?*
WHY? BECAUSE I WON'T SIT BACK AND RELY ON THE WULFENBACH FORCES TO PROTECT US?
NOT THAT LONG AGO, *THEY* WERE THE ONES *ATTACKING* US.
AN HOUR FROM NOW, THEY COULD ATTACK US AGAIN.
NO. THIS IS *MY* TOWN.
I'LL PROTECT IT.
I...DO TRUST *GIL*, BUT I DON'T KNOW HOW MUCH I CAN TRUST THE *RULER OF THE EMPIRE*.
I WANT US STRONG ENOUGH THAT *NOBODY* CAN TAKE US.
...THAT'S VERY ASTUTE, MY LADY.
DON'T SOUND SO *SURPRISED*, PAL!
SHE'S BEEN LEARNING FROM THE *BEST!*
ennui-
ANGST-
DREAD-
ZAP
sigh
HM? YOU OKAY?
I...I GUESS.
I JUST WONDER HOW MANY *OTHER* GIRLS WORRY ABOUT WHETHER OR NOT IT'S SMART TO REALLY TRUST THEIR...
AH, YOU KNOW, THE GUYS THEY...
UM... PROBABLY *ALL* OF THEM?
BUT *MINE* HAS AN *ARMY!*

ON CASTLE WULFENBACH—
THERE! I THINK YOU'VE GOT THE HANG OF IT NOW!
OH, GOLLY, DO YOU REALLY THINK SO?
WELL, NO.
BUT IF ACTING THE SYCOPHANTIC TOADY WILL GET ME BACK TO AGATHA FASTER...
OH, I'LL GET YOU THERE FAST—
CANNONEERS!
YES?
SIR! WE'VE CAUGHT A—
A—
WELL, WE'RE NOT REALLY SURE WHAT IT IS.
...YOU'RE KIDDING.
REALLY! HANGING FROM THE BOTTOM OF THE GONDOLA!
HE INSISTS IT'S A MATTER OF LIFE OR DEATH!
tsk. YOU KNOW I'LL BE OF MORE USE IN ONE PIECE...
YEAH, YEAH— BUT I DON'T HAVE TO LIKE IT.
YOU! GILGAMESH WULFENBACH!
I MUST SPEAK WITH YOU!
IT'S OF THE UTMOST IMPORTANCE!
ZIP!
WHOA!
WHA—
IT'S ABOUT A BOOK!
BORIS?
WAIT A MINUTE— YOU?!
HOW DID YOU GET HERE?!
YOU KNOW THIS—?
HE SHOULD BE ROTTING IN A CELL IN STURMHALTEN!
BECAUSE OF HIS RIDICULOUS ANTICS,
THE DEEP LIBRARY IS INFESTED WITH GIANT SMUDGE BEETLES!
GRAB
NOOOO!
—AND IT HAPPENED WHILE HE WAS COLLECTING VILE, SCURRILOUS STORIES ABOUT MY FAMILY, I MIGHT ADD!
OOOH. HE SOUNDS WELL INFORMED!
LET HIM DOWN, BORIS. I'LL LISTEN TO HIM.

...AND THUS, THE GREAT WOLF WAS *SLAIN*—

AND PEACE RETURNED TO THE KINGDOM.

THE END! (sniff)

...I'VE NEVER HEARD THIS MORONIC STORY IN MY *LIFE*.

Z

—AND YOU'RE SAYING *MY FATHER* TOLD IT TO YOU?

YES! HE SAID IT'S IN THE BOOK! THE ONE IN YOUR LIBRARY!

THE ONE BY *MASAT!*

HE SAID YOU'D LET ME SEE IT!

THERE *IS* NO SUCH BOOK!

AND THAT STORY MAKES *NO SENSE!*

IT MAKES SENSE TO *ME*.

WHAT? *SERIOUSLY?*

YES. THE PLAN WAS FOR LUCREZIA TO GET CLOSE ENOUGH TO WASP THE BARON.

SHE...SHE MUST HAVE MANAGED IT—BUT I CAN'T IMAGINE *HOW*.

WHAT? MY *FATHER?!* BUT SPARKS—

THEY'VE DEVELOPED A NEW STRAIN.

"THEY?!" THEY *WHO?!*

WELL, *MOSTLY* A SPARK CALLED GOTTMURG SNARLANTZ...

AND *YOU KNEW ABOUT THIS!*

YES! COME ON! *QUICKLY!* I'LL—

POW! POW! POW!
HOLD YOUR FIRE!
SLAM!
SIR! ARE YOU ALL RIGHT?
I'M FINE, CAPTAIN. LEAVE HIM ALONE.
YOU IDIOT!
ARE YOU TRYING TO COMMIT SUICIDE?!
YOU KNOW I WOULDN'T DO THAT TO HER.
ANYWAY, LUCREZIA'S ALREADY GOT TO AGATHA, REMEMBER?
—AND I'M THE ONLY ONE WHO KNOWS ENOUGH TO HAVE A CHANCE OF BREAKING HER FREE!
ALL RIGHT! I KNOW!
HAVE YOU ALREADY FORGOTTEN HOW MUCH TROUBLE WE WENT THROUGH TO KEEP YOU ALIVE?
HOW DARE YOU RISK YOURSELF AND HER BY ACTING SO STUPID!
SMAK!
OW! LET ME UP! WE'VE GOT TO GET YOU OUT OF HERE— QUICKLY!
GET ME OUT OF HERE?
NO.
I STAY HERE.
I WANT YOU TO STICK CLOSE TO AGATHA.
YOU'RE AN OPPORTUNISTIC SERPENT UP TO YOUR EARS IN TREACHERY AND INTRIGUE—
SO YOU SHOULD BE ABLE TO SPOT, AND DEAL WITH, ANY HIDDEN THREATS.
—AND YES, TRY TO FIND A WAY TO GET RID OF LUCREZIA.
I'LL USE THE EMPIRE TO CLEAR OUT THE OBVIOUS ATTACKS.
I CAN'T JOIN YOU UNTIL WE'VE GOT THINGS BACK UNDER CONTROL.
YOU WON'T BE ANY USE TO US AT ALL IF YOU STAY HERE AND GET WASPED.
I REALLY DON'T THINK—
SIR! THEY'VE FOUND THE BARON!
HE'S ALIVE!
I KNEW IT!

TIME TO GO!
WAIT! YOU'RE JUST GUESSING, RIGHT?
ABOUT MY FATHER?
YOU ARE, AREN'T YOU?
YES... NO!
NO! THAT IDIOT STORYTELLER—IT'S OBVIOUS THAT YOUR FATHER HAS USED HIM TO GET A MESSAGE TO YOU!
IF HE'S BEEN WASPED, HE WON'T BE ABLE TO TELL ANYONE ABOUT IT DIRECTLY. HE SHOULDN'T BE ABLE TO TELL ANYONE AT ALL.
BUT YOUR FATHER IS... EXTRAORDINARY. IT'S LIKE THE USUAL RULES DON'T APPLY TO HIM.
MAYBE SHE DIDN'T GET HIM COMPLETELY, I...I DON'T KNOW...
BUT I'M NOT GOING TO WAIT FOR HER TO GET YOU TOO, JUST SO I CAN FIND OUT FOR SURE.
IF YOU'RE RIGHT ABOUT THIS—
THERE MAY NOT BE MUCH YOU CAN DO ABOUT THAT.
HAVEN'T YOU BEEN LISTENING TO THE THINGS I'VE BEEN TELLING YOU?
I STUDIED WITH LUCREZIA!
SHE SHOWED ME ALL KINDS OF THINGS!
—AND I THINK I'VE WORKED OUT A FORMULA TO KEEP WASPS FROM GAINING CONTROL.
WHAT?! THEN WHY HAVEN'T YOU—
I'VE BEEN KIND OF BUSY LATELY!
SO LISTEN. AS FAR AS I KNOW, THERE WAS ONLY ONE OF THE SPARK WASPS.
IT SHOULD TAKE SOME TIME FOR LUCREZIA TO MAKE NEW ONES, BUT WE CAN'T BE SURE OF ANYTHING WHEN IT COMES TO HER.
I'LL TELL YOU HOW TO MAKE IT. IF WE GET SEPARATED, YOU GET TO A LAB AND DOSE YOURSELF AS SOON AS YOU CAN.
YOU HAVE GOT TO BE KIDDING ME.
HOW DO I KNOW IT WON'T JUST TURN ME INTO A TOAD OR SOMETHING?
...WELL, I SUPPOSE YOU'LL JUST HAVE TO GO AGAINST YOUR BETTER JUDGEMENT AND TRUST ME.
AH, SEE, NOW, THAT'S THE HARD PART.

BA
OKAY, YOU KNOW WHAT?
I NEVER KNEW WHAT I HAD DONE TO MAKE YOU HATE ME SO MUCH,
BUT I THINK I'VE FINALLY FIGURED IT OUT.
THAT TIME WE WERE CAUGHT SNEAKING INTO THE RECORDS VAULT?
I'LL BET THAT'S WHEN THE BARON TOLD YOU THAT YOU WERE HIS SON.
HE PROBABLY WARNED YOU AGAINST ME, TOO—TOLD YOU ALL ABOUT MY FAMILY, AND WHAT TREACHEROUS BACKSTABBERS WE ALL ARE...
OH? AND THAT'S NOT TRUE?
OF COURSE IT'S TRUE!
BUT WE WERE—
WELL, WE BOTH WANTED TO FIND SOMETHING EXCITING ABOUT YOUR PAST!
IT WAS JUST FOR FUN! HOW WAS I SUPPOSED TO KNOW HOW IT WOULD LOOK TO THE BARON?
NO WONDER I GOT THROWN OFF THE CASTLE!
WELL—
—AND ALL THAT TIME IN PARIS—
"WHEN YOU WERE WALLOWING IN DEBAUCHERY WITH YOUR DOXIES, TARTS AND PIRATES—"
VOTED MOST LIKELY
YOU WERE TRYING TO CONVINCE ME THAT YOU WERE A DISGUSTING, SWINISH, LECHEROUS, DRUNKEN SOT.
WELL, I WANT YOU TO KNOW, IT WORKED.
WELL DONE!

...FINE. I'LL... I'LL TRUST YOU THIS ONCE.
JUST...SHUT UP ABOUT IT FOR NOW.
WE'VE GOT TO THINK—AND WE DON'T HAVE THE TIME—
WE CAN'T JUST RUN STRAIGHT TO THE NEAREST DIRIGIBLE BAY...
WHY NOT?
"MY FATHER IS A BRILLIANT STRATEGIST. HE CAN OUT THINK ANYBODY.
HE'S ALWAYS AT LEAST FIVE STEPS AHEAD OF HIS ENEMIES.
"—EXCEPT POSSIBLY LUCREZIA."
TRUE. SO IF HE'S UNDER HER CONTROL—"
HANGAR BAYS 100-13
NEITHER OF THEM WOULD BE STUPID ENOUGH TO LET IT SHOW. WHOA!
THIS WAY. YES—THEY'LL BE CAREFUL. SUBTLE.
WE DON'T KNOW HOW LONG HE'S ALREADY BEEN HERE.
711
NO BANANA
UH OH. PEOPLE WERE BEING CALLED AWAY FROM THE OPERATIONS ROOM—
...NOT GOOD. THEN WE HAVE NO WAY OF KNOWING WHAT ORDERS MY FATHER HAS ALREADY GIVEN—
EVEN UN-WASPED HE'D PROBABLY HAVE YOU SHOT.
YEAH, I GET THAT A LOT.
FOR WHAT IT'S WORTH, YOU'VE EARNED IT. HE KNOWS YOU'RE DANGEROUS.
GREAT. AND LUCREZIA'S ALREADY SHOT ME ONCE—
SO TELL ME AGAIN WHY WE'RE NOT LEAVING?
WE ARE LEAVING—
BUT I'LL BET EVERY HANGAR BAY HAS GUARDS BY NOW, WAITING TO GRAB YOU.
...MAYBE BOTH OF US.
WE STILL HAVE TO GO—
BUT NOW WE'RE ESCAPING.

GIL!
WHAT ARE YOU DOING?!
I WENT TO GET COFFEE, AND WHEN I GOT TO OPERATIONS, THEY SAID YOU'D JUST BOLTED OUT OF THERE WITH NO EXPLANATION!
AAAAH! NOOO! NOT YOU!
OH MY GOSH! OH MY GOSH!
I'D KNOW THAT GIRLISH SCREAM ANYWHERE!
IT'S PRINCE "HOW DARE YOU!"
I CAN'T BELIEVE IT! IT'S REALLY YOU!
I THOUGHT YOU'D JUMPED TO YOUR DEATH!
OH, WOW!
WULFENBACH, WHAT IS SHE DOING HERE?
DOESN'T YOUR EMPIRE SHOOT PIRATES?
SHOOT HER NOW!
RIGHT NOW!
I KNOW, I KNOW. I KEEP MEANING TO.
I'M AMAZED MY FATHER HASN'T—
AH.
OOOH, I'VE MISSED YOU, ME PROUD BEAUTY!
HEE HEE! YARRRR!
DuPREE! COME WITH US.
YAY!
HEY, DO YOU STILL HAVE THOSE LITTLE SCARS?
C'MON! LEMME SEE!
SHE'S COMING WITH US? WHY?!
...BECAUSE I
TO GET WASPED.
THINK ABOUT IT. CAN YOU IMAGINE WHAT SHE'D BE LIKE IF SHE WERE WORKING FOR LUCREZIA?
SO SHOOT HER!
HA!
SO FUNNY!

SOON—
SO IF WE'RE NOT GOING TO THE HANGARS, WHERE *ARE* WE GOING?
TO MY LAB.
WITH ANY LUCK, NO ONE WILL EXPECT US TO GO *THERE*, AND—
DERE HYU IZ!
VOLE! HOW DID YOU *FIND* US?!
tch. HYU CHEELDRUN TINKS HYU IZ SO *SCHNEEKY!*
DOT'S CUTE—BUY HYU GOTS *BIGGER PROBLEMS*, KIDDO.
HYU POPPA IS *ALIVE AFTER ALL!*
HE GOTS DE SECURITY FORCES RUNNINK ALL OVER DE PLACE—LOOKINK FOR *HYU!*
HYU IZ TO BE DETAINED—
PRINZE *SCHTURMVURAUZ* IZ TO BE DETAINED—
OOH, AREN'T *YOU* POPULAR?
shh—*WAIT*...
THIS COULD BE *BAD*...
ENNYBODDY WHO HAZ EVEN *TALKED* TO HYU IZ TO BE DETAINED!
...AND ARE *YOU* HERE TO..."*DETAIN*" US?
HO! *NO VAY*, BOSS!
HY VORKS FOR *HYU* NOW, *REMEMBER?*
HY IZ HERE TO *HELP HYU OUT!*
HYU IZ GOINK AGAINST HYU POPPA?
WHOO! DOT'S GONNA BE SOME *VAR!*
MESSY, TERRIBLE, CIVIL VAR!
DE EMPIRE VILL BE IN *FLAMES!*
DE PIPPLE VILL BE *CRUSHED* BETVEEN HYU!
HYU VILL UNLEASH AN *OCEAN* OV BLOOD!
DIS IS MORE DEN HY EFFER COULD HEFF HOPED FOR!
IT VILL BE *GLORIOUS!*
WHUMP!

—UND PUT EFFRYVUN WHO IZ STILL ALIFE ON DOES BEEG SPIKES...
DEN VE KEN BURN DE FIELDS,
...UND DANCE IN DE BONES! YEZ!
UND DEN...MUTTER, MUTTER...
ARE YOU ACTUALLY LISTENING TO ANY OF THIS?
NOT REALLY. IF THAT'S WHAT'S KEEPING HIM FROM TURNING US IN, THEN FINE.
HE'S OBVIOUSLY ENJOYING HIMSELF.
—BUT IF YOU'RE WORRIED, WE COULD ALWAYS JUST SURRENDER RIGHT NOW.
IF YOU'RE RIGHT ABOUT ALL THIS, I'LL JUST GET WASPED.
YOU'LL PROBABLY WIND UP DEAD EITHER WAY, BUT AT LEAST WE'D AVOID A CIVIL WAR.
...BUT I AM HOPING WE CAN AVOID ONE WITHOUT GETTING YOU KILLED—
SO LET'S JUST WORRY ABOUT ONE THING AT A TIME.
FIRST, TO MY LAB.
YEAH, BUT... WHAT MAKES YOU THINK THEY WON'T BE WAITING THERE?
OH. WE'RE GOING TO MY SECRET LAB.
"THERE ARE ALWAYS CONSTRUCTION CREWS DOING SOME KIND OF WORK ON THE CASTLE.
WHEN ENOUGH CREWS ARE WORKING AT ONCE, IT'S PRETTY EASY TO ALTER THE BLUEPRINTS WITHOUT ANYONE NOTICING."
I'VE GOT A WHOLE SECTION SEALED OFF FROM THE MAIN SHIP.
WOW. THAT'S...THAT'S ACTUALLY PRETTY COOL.
ISN'T IT, THOUGH? AH. HERE WE ARE.
KLANGK
OKAY, COME ON UP!
IT'S ALL CLEAR!
SKREEEK!
AAAAH!
GLOMPH

ZOING! GOOD TO SEE YOU!
WHIRRYU BEEEE?
I TOLD YOU I'D BE BUSY— HOW ARE THE PATIENTS?
NODED.
AH! FINAL HEALING IS PROGRESSING BEAUTIFULLY!
ANOTHER DAY OR TWO AND THEY'LL BE GOOD AS NEW!
YOP!
IZ MEESTER PONCH!
GREAT HEAVENS.
UND MEEZTREZ JUDY! HY TOT DEY VAS DEAD.
VELL HOWZABOUT DOT.
NOW LET'S GET GOING! THIS ONE OVER HERE IS ONLY EXPERIMENTAL—
WHERE'S THE GAS BAG?
IT DOESN'T HAVE ONE! I SAID IT'S EXPERIMENTAL.
SO...SO IT'S SOME KIND OF FALLING MACHINE?
WELL, NOT EXACTLY, BUT—
THIS CONTRAPTION WON'T FLY AT ALL!
SCIENCE SAYS IT WILL!
THEN SCIENCE CAN FLY IT!
tsk. I ASSURE YOU, EVEN IF IT DOESN'T "FLY," EXACTLY, IT SHOULD REACH THE GROUND IN ONE PIECE LONG BEFORE IT EXPLODES.
WELL, I THINK SO, ANYWAY. I HAVEN'T ACTUALLY TESTED IT SINCE I
HERE ARE THE CONTROLS! THEY'RE PRETTY SIMPLE. CAN YOU RUN A FOUR GEAR LANDWALKER?
UM, ONCE, AT THE UNIVERSITY, I—
PERFECT! BUT INSTEAD OF WALKING, THINK OF IT AS SKATING.
BUT I'VE NEVER—
YOU SHOULDN'T HAVE TO WORRY ABOUT ANY OF THESE—
THEY'RE JUST FUEL, ALTIMETER, LIGHTS, BRAKES, AND THE GIANT CLAW.
WAIT A MINUTE—
WHY TELL ME...OH. OH, NO!
YOU CANNOT SERIOUSLY BE PLANNING TO—
YOU ARE! FOR SOME POINTLESS, NO DOUBT PENNY DREADFUL-INDUCED DELUSION OF NOBLE SACRIFICE, YOU'RE PLANNING TO STAY HERE!
WHY?!

WHY, AH, I HAVE NO IDEA WHAT YOU'RE...
DON'T EVEN TRY TO PULL THAT ON ME!
WHAT DO YOU THINK YOU CAN ACCOMPLISH HERE?
HAVE YOU EVEN CONSIDERED HOW DANGEROUS A SPARK OF YOUR CALIBER WILL BE WHEN YOU'RE WORKING FOR THE OTHER?
IT'S BAD ENOUGH THAT SHE'S GOT YOUR FATHER!
WE...DON'T KNOW THAT...
IF SHE GETS YOU, TOO—THE REST OF US MIGHT AS WELL GIVE UP AND BURN EUROPA TO THE GROUND OURSELVES!
EVEN IF YOU HAD ALREADY USED MY FORMULA—
EVEN IF WE WERE COMPLETELY SURE IT WOULD WORK—
STAYING HERE WOULD STILL BE SUICIDE!
—AND I HAVEN'T EVEN SHOWN YOU MY NOTES, YET!
PLUS, I DO NOT BELIEVE THIS THING CAN EVEN HOVER, LET ALONE FLY!
OF COURSE IT CAN'T HOVER!
A-HA!
LISTEN, YOU IDIOT!
LOTS OF THINGS FLY WITHOUT GASBAGS.
YOU HAVE ABSOLUTELY NO GRASP OF AERONAUTICS, DO YOU?
CRASH!
YOU'LL BE FINE.
I AM NOT LEAVING YOU HERE TO GET CAPTURED.
WULFENBACH! WE MEET AGAIN! YES, AT LAST I HAVE FOUND YOU—
AND YOUR DEGENERATE CLONE!
HIS WHAT?! HOW DARE YOU, YOU—
OOOH! PERFECT!

CURSES! FOILED AGAIN!
WH— WHAT?
WE MUST FLEE—FOR IT IS NONE OTHER THAN:
OTHAR TRYGGVASSEN
Gentleman Adventurer
VANQUISHER OF EEEEVIL!
HEY NOW! YOU MAKE IT SOUND ABSURD!
WE WILL MAKE A DARING ESCAPE IN MY AMAZING FLYING MACHINE!
NOT THE FLYING MACHINE! NOT THE FLYING MACHINE!
I THINK NOT, VILLAIN!
I STILL NEED TO DRAG YOU BACK TO THE BARON— OOF!
OOF! WHAT IS THE MATTER WITH YOU?!
DON'T WORRY! OTHAR HERE IS A MASTER OF ESCAPE!
CLICK-
CLICK!
HE'S ALWAYS FALLING OUT OF AIRSHIPS AND STUFF—
SO IF YOU'RE WITH HIM—
WHAT—
THE—
I KNOW YOU'LL GET AWAY!
BZT
OH, NO.
OH—AND LET ME KNOW HOW HE DOES IT!
DAAAAAAAAAAAAAAAHH!!
CLANG!

...
DOT NO GOOT SCHNEAK!
hmf. HO, VELL, LET'S GET GOIN'.
EEF WE'S GUN' START A CIVIL VAR, VE GOTS TO GET CRACKIN'.
YEEES— ABOUT THAT—
SHOVE
AAAAAAAAAAH!
WHAT DID YOU DO THAT FOR?
WHAT?
OH. HE SHOULD BE FINE.
THEY HAVEN'T EVEN GOT THE ENGINE STARTED YET.
SEE? THEY'RE STILL RIGHT BELOW US.
HEY!
Vip
NOW WHAT? DON'T TELL ME YOU'RE MAD THAT YOU DIDN'T GET TO PUSH HIM—
I...I LIKED THAT ONE!
YOU... LIKE HIM?
YOU... LIKE... YOU–?!
WAHAHAHAHA! OF COURSE YOU DO!
HE'S A BLOODTHIRSTY, TREACHEROUS KILLING MACHINE!
OH, THIS IS JUST PRICELESS!
BANG HAS A BOOOYFRIEND! hee hee!

hmf. YEAH, WELL, ***YOU*** SHOULD TALK. TWERP.

WHAT ABOUT ALL THIS TROUBLE ***YOU'RE*** CAUSING OVER THAT ***HETERODYNE*** WENCH?

HMM. POINT TAKEN.

SO LET ME TAKE A LOOK AT THIS ***FORMULA.***

DuPREE, YOU START CLEARING A SPACE ON CHEMICAL TABLE THREE, AND GET ME—

OH, NO YOU DON'T. ***I*** STILL WORK FOR YOUR ***FATHER***—

AND IT SOUNDS LIKE ***HE*** WANTS YOU BROUGHT IN ***NOW.***

OH, I ***CAN'T BELIEVE*** IT.

OH, YOU'D ***BETTER*** BELIEVE IT.

NOW ***GET MOVING!***

snap

NOT ***YOU***— STURMVORAUS' NOTES. THEY'RE ***ENCRYPTED.***

WELL, ISN'T THAT JUST ***TOO BAD***—

DuPREE.

PLEASE.

I NEED YOU TO STAY HERE, WITH ME—

WHUMP!

AND LET ME WORK!

BOOT!

WHOA!

SERIOUSLY, DuPREE—THIS IS *VERY*—
OH!
SILVER OF VIXONITE!

I THOUGHT I WAS GOING TO HAVE TO MAKE MORE OF THIS FROM *SCRATCH!*
THAT'S GOING TO MAKE THIS A *LOT* EASIER!

HEY!
WOOP!
CAREFUL! THIS FORMULA'S DIFFICULT ENOUGH WITHOUT YOU *BREAKING STUFF!*

HOW DO YOU *KNOW THAT?*
I THOUGHT YOU SAID YOU COULDN'T *READ* THOSE NOTES!
WAK!

THUP!
I SAID THEY WERE *ENCRYPTED*.
I DIDN'T SAY I *COULDN'T READ THEM.*
OH, YEAH? WELL—

NOW, WOULD YOU SEE IF WE HAVE ANY DISTILLATION OF MONAHAN'S VENEFIROUS MUS ELIXIR LEFT?
BOOT!

I'LL DISTILL *YOU!*
—AND *LOOK* AT ME WHEN I'M TRYING TO KILL YOU!

AH, *PERFECT!* THANKS!
AND NEXT TO *THAT,* THERE SHOULD BE A BOTTLE OF—
SMEK!

CALIXIA OIL! THAT'S RIGHT!
HEY, YOU'RE GETTING BETTER AT THIS!
SMEK!
REMEMBER THAT TIME YOU GAVE ME CONCENTRATED PELLICAX'S TWIST INSTEAD OF ST. MICHAEL'S TOES
SHIP BLEW UP?

SLAM!
A *TABLE?!*
NO NO *NO!*
I'VE ALREADY GOT ONE OF THOSE!

HM. THAT PART SOUNDS TRICKY—
LOOK, I'LL ADMIT THIS IS OCCASIONALLY FUN,
BUT THIS IS NOT THE TIME, OKAY?
KLANG!
OH, IT'S ALWAYS THE TIME, YOU—
ZOING?
FWOMP!
WHA—!
GOTONE! TOLDYUIT BEGOOD!
YES, YES. YOU WERE RIGHT I WAS WRONG.
EEEEEE!
HEY! CHEATING! THIS IS CHEATING!
THIS... WHAT IS THIS THING?
OH, UH... I BUILT IT FOR ZOING A LONG TIME AGO.
IZFOR PICKINGUP GORLZ!
IT'S FOR WHAT?!
WELL, WHEN I WAS A KID, WE HEARD SOME OF THE OLDER GUYS TALKING,
BUT WE WERE KIND OF...UM... UNCLEAR ON THE CONCEPT, AND, WELL...
ITWORKZ! ITWORKZ!
THAT IS SO JUST LIKE YOU... SOOOO PATHETIC.
ARGH— JUST STRAP HER DOWN SOMEWHERE, OKAY?

...SERIOUSLY PATHETIC.
I ASSURE YOU, THAT TABLE IS PURELY FOR MEDICAL PURPOSES.
THAT'S WHAT I MEANT! AND WHAT ARE YOU WORKING ON THAT'S SO IMPORTANT, ANYWAY?
2¢ Deposit
WELL, I'LL ADMIT THAT I'M JUST FOLLOWING THE FORMULA—I HAVEN'T HAD TIME TO STUDY THE THEORY BEHIND IT IN DETAIL,
BUT THE RESULT SHOULD BE SOMETHING THAT WILL PROTECT US AGAINST SLAVER WASP INFECTION.
BUT—THOSE NOTES—"STURMVORAUS?" THAT GUY'S THE PRINCE FROM STURMHALTEN?
AND YOU'RE MIXING UP SOME WEIRD THING YOU GOT FROM HIM?
I THINK I REALLY AM GOING TO HAVE TO KILL YOU.
STURMHALTEN'S THE CENTER OF THIS WHOLE MESS WITH THE OTHER!
APPARENTLY, THE ROYAL FAMILY THERE WAS NECK DEEP IN IT!
YES. I KNOW.
THAT'S WHY I THINK THIS HAS A CHANCE OF WORKING.
ANYWAY, I DON'T HAVE MUCH CHOICE.
THERE'S A... POSSIBILITY...THAT MY FATHER HAS BEEN INFECTED.

WAIT. YOU THINK *YOUR FATHER*—THE BIGGEST SPARK IN THE LOONEY BIN—HAS BEEN WASPED?
SINCE WHEN IS THAT EVEN *POSSIBLE?*
SINCE THOSE KNIGHTS OF JOVE FIGURED OUT HOW TO INFECT US.
THEY'VE BEEN WORKING FOR THE OTHER SINCE BEFORE SHE MARRIED BILL HETERODYNE,
AND NOW THAT SHE'S BACK, THEY'RE MAKING THEIR MOVE.
BASED ON WHAT HE ALREADY KNEW ABOUT WASPS, AND WHAT LUCREZIA APPARENTLY TAUGHT HIM, STURMVORAUS HAS BEEN ABLE TO—
UM—
DuPREE—ARE YOU LISTENING TO *ANYTHING* I'M SAYING?
OH, *I'M LISTENING.*
WHUMP!
YOU'VE BECOME WEIRDLY INFATUATED WITH THIS GIRL WHO'S PROBABLY THE OTHER—
AND YOU'VE BEEN OFF WITH HER, GETTING ALL CHUMMY WITH PRINCE SQUEALY, A WET BLANKET YOU ALWAYS *HATED* BEFORE...
AND WHO IS CURRENTLY ONE OF THE PEOPLE HEADING YOUR FATHER'S "MOST WANTED" LIST—
AND WHO KNOWS ALL ABOUT HOW SLAVER WASPS WORK.
NOW, YOU'RE MIXING UP SOME FREAKY POTION HE CAME UP WITH—
AND YOU EXPECT *ME* TO *DRINK IT.*
DOES *THAT* ABOUT COVER IT?
BOK!
YES,
OOF
AND *NO.*

OW!
OW!
ENOUGH OF THIS.
I DON'T CARE IF YOU BELIEVE ME OR NOT, THIS IS *IMPORTANT*.
I *NEED* YOU TO STAY *FREE*.
GUG GUG
ER—SORRY ABOUT THAT,
BUT *SEE?* I'M GOING TO DRINK IT TOO!
KOFF!
PAH!

ASSUMING I GOT THE DOSAGE RIGHT, THERE SHOULD BE ENOUGH HERE TO PROTECT BOTH OF US—
...AND ZOING, *YOU* DON'T—
MEEEEP!
NNARRRGH!
I KNEW SHE'D GOT TO YOU!
I SHOULD *KILL* YOU *NOW!*
I—NO! I THINK THIS IS *SUPPOSED* TO HAPPEN—
WAIT A SECOND—
LET ME CHECK THE NOTES—
UM— HERE WE GO— TABLE H: *"TEMPORARY SIDE EFFECTS—"*
...AH! I SEE!

MEANWHILE—
AAAAAAAH!
KACHAK KACHAK
ACHAKA
choff
KLONK
choff
choff
CALM YOURSELF!
THE FLYING MACHINE IS WORKING—
NOT ENOUGH! WE'RE STILL FALLING!
—THEN PANIC IS A LUXURY WE CANNOT AFFORD.
...OKAY, FINE.
I'M POSITIVELY SERENE.
NOW, DO YOU KNOW ANYTHING ABOUT THESE THINGS?
DON'T YOU?
NO! I WOULDN'T GO NEAR A THING LIKE THIS WITH A TEN FOOT HAMMER!
THERE'S NO GASBAG! IT'S—IT'S LIKE SOME GIANT CREEPY FLAPPING BUG—¡
...THAT'S SERENE, IS IT?
I REALLY DON'T LIKE FLYING!
A-HAH!
K-RUNCH!
HEH HEH. GOT HIM! PRETTY SCHNEEKY, YAH?
AAAH! NO! HE'S THE ONE WULFENBACH SAID WOULD GET US OUT OF THIS!

HOOF!
SOK!
HO HO! YOU WON'T TAKE ME DOWN THAT EASILY, EVILDOER!
HOW—
HA! A MERE CHAIN IS NOTHING FOR AN ADVENTURER SUCH AS MYSELF!
WHAT? NO! I THOUGHT HE'D BROKEN YOUR BACK!
OH, THAT.
SPECIAL TROUSERS.
WHAT?!
VERY HEROIC.
ANYWAY, COULD YOU PLEASE—
UM—
PEH. HYU GOODY TWO-SHOES TYPES IZ ALL VIT DE BEEG MOUTHS.
HY TEK HYU DOWN JUST FINE, HYU SEE.
BAF!
STOP!
HITTING!
HIM!
I THINK NOT, CREATURE OF EVIL!
OH, FOR-
FINE! DON'T LET ME BOTHER YOU!
AT LEAST NOW I HAVE BOTH HANDS FREE TO WORK.
LET'S SEE...
TCH. SO CRUDE-
ALL POWER AND NO FINESSE.
HMM... BUT I GUESS IT IS RATHER BRILLIANT, IN ITS WAY...
ITS CRUDE, SMUG, IRRITATING, LOWLIFE, DEBAUCHED WAY-
WRENCH!
GRAAAARH!
BAF!
THANK YOU.
NOW THEN, ABOUT THIS FALLING BUSINESS—
DONE!
VROOOOOOOKACHAKACHAKAC
SAY—YOU'RE BETTER AT THIS THAN I'D THOUGHT!
WE'LL MAKE A HERO OUT OF YOU YET, YOUNG VILLAIN!
I HATE HATE HATE HATE HATE HATE FLYING.

HALT!
SURRENDER, AND YOU'LL BE TAKEN SAFELY INTO CUSTODY UNTIL WE CAN SEND YOU BACK TO YOUR BARON.
RESIST, AND WE'LL SHOOT!
NEVER FEAR, GOOD PEOPLE! I AM NO AGENT OF WULFENBACH—
I AM...
OTHAR TRYGGVASSEN
GENTLEMAN ADVENTURER!
OH, SURE, THAT'LL—
WOW! REALLY?
THE OTHAR?
WE'LL TAKE YOU TO THE LADY HETERODYNE RIGHT AWAY!
YEAH! I BET SHE'LL BE THRILLED!
...
OF COURSE SHE WILL!
OH, AND YOU'LL WANT TO DISPOSE OF THIS...
HOLY KATZENJAMMER! IT'S VOLE!
GET A MONSTER WAGON OVER HERE, ON THE DOUBLE!
HUH. I ALWAYS HEARD THAT OTHAR TRYGGVASSEN HAD SPUNKY GIRL SIDEKICKS.
hmf. WELL, ORDINARILY, I ASSURE YOU—
I AM NOT THIS OAF'S SIDEKICK. I AM THE ST—er—
I AM...THE CHIEF ADVISOR TO YOUR LADY HETERODYNE.
YEAH? WELL, WE'LL LET HER DECIDE THAT.

HEYA! IT AIN'T MUCH, BUT IT'S HOT!
OOOH! THANK YOU, SQUINALDO! YOUR CONCOCTIONS ARE ALWAYS A TREAT!
HOY! HOLD ON!
EH?
WAIT FOR EVERYONE ELSE!
OH! OF COURSE!
TO THE LADY HETERODYNE! ONCE AGAIN, WE ARE FREE!
HUZZAH!
AH! DELICIOUS!
...AND IT ISN'T EVEN POISONED!
tsk—I AM A NEW MAN!
PSYCH! SLOW POISON!
ALREADY DEAD! BURN!
SO, WHAT ARE YOUR PLANS, PROFESSOR?
TO TELL THE TRUTH, I AM NOT SURE.
I NEVER REALLY THOUGHT I WOULD GET OUT OF HERE.

PROFESSOR!

AH! FRAULEIN SNAUG!

ASTONISHING! YOU'RE ALIVE!

WHEE! AND YOU'RE STILL A TWISTED MOCKERY OF LIFE, SIR!

SAUCE!

OH, GEEZ! IT'S HIM.

WHAT? A PROBLEM?

UGH. IT'S THAT MORLOCK GUY.
HE'S JUST SUCH A TOTAL SPAZ AND IT'S OBVIOUS HE'S STUPID IN LOVE WITH ME.
HE'S SO RIDICULOUSLY USELESS.
YOU...YOU'RE TALKING ABOUT HERR VON ZINZER?!
LISTEN UP, PEOPLE!
THE CASTLE'S GIVEN ME A MAP OF THE TOWN'S OLD DEFENSES.
MOST OF 'EM ARE BROKEN OR DISCONNECTED, BUT IT DOESN'T SOUND LIKE ANYTHING WE CAN'T HANDLE.
ALSO, THE CASTLE'S PROMISED NOT TO KILL ANY MORE OF US FOR FUN, SO WE CAN COME BACK TO BURY OUR DEAD ONCE THIS IS ALL OVER.
NOW, LET'S HEAD DOWN INTO TOWN AND GET TO WORK.
HUH. BURY THE DEAD? THAT SEEM LIKE A WASTE...
SURELY WE COULD USE THEM TO—

NO!
BAF
WHAT?
YOU—
R-79
YOU MADBOYS CAN DO WHATEVER SICK STUFF YOU WANT ON YOUR OWN TURF—
BUT ANY ONE OF THEM COULD HAVE BEEN YOU, OR ME!
WE'LL TREAT THEM WITH RESPECT!
AH. OF COURSE.
SORRY.
WHERE DO WE GO FIRST?
HMMM, YES...
I CAN SEE HOW THAT MUST BE VERY EMBARRASSING FOR YOU.

CASTLE WULFENBACH—
uhhhrrgh...
jeez, bang, why'd you have to hit me so *hard*—?
UH—
WHAT—?
snif
snif
SCREEE!
GROWR!
SSSSSS!
SSSSSS!
AH...IT IS AS I *FEARED*.

THERE IS NO LONGER ANY DOUBT. THE GIRL IS CLEARLY—
NO!
sigh. PLEASE REFRAIN FROM ANY MORE FOOLISHNESS.
YOU WILL ONLY BE CONFINED UNTIL I CAN GIVE THIS PROBLEM MY FULL ATTENTION.
TAKE HIM TO THE RED LEVEL.
PLACE HIM UNDER AIRTIGHT, CODE FIVE RESTRAINT.
FORCE LEVEL PARAMETERS?
TRY NOT TO KILL HIM, BUT HE MUST NOT BE ALLOWED TO ESCAPE.
AND GILGAMESH— MY SON— YOU HAVE MY WORD—
NO MATTER WHAT HAPPENS, I WILL DO EVERYTHING IN MY POWER TO HELP YOU.
BUT NOW I MUST DEAL WITH THE HETERODYNE GIRL AND HER ACCOMPLICES.
THEY, AT LEAST, CANNOT BE ALLOWED TO LIVE.

FATHER, NO!
AGATHA DOESN'T EVEN HAVE THAT TECHNOLOGY!
SHE COULDN'T HAVE WASPED ME!
SHE DIDN'T HAVE TO.
YOU WERE INFECTED BEFORE YOU EVEN MET HER.
I...
NO. THAT'S NOT...NOT POSSIBLE.
...IS IT?
THESE DOCUMENTS WERE FOUND IN A SECRET LAB IN STURMHALTEN.
ACCORDING TO THEM, YOU WERE INFECTED IN PARIS.
BUT...BUT STURMVORAUS SAID THE SPARK WASPS WERE—
I WARNED YOU AGAINST STURMVORAUS YEARS AGO!
HE AND THAT HETERODYNE GIRL HAVE PLAYED YOU FOR A FOOL!
BUT...BUT WHEN COULD HE HAVE—?
I WOULD ASSUME IT WAS DONE THROUGH AN AGENT.
THAT FAMILY NEVER DOES THEIR OWN DIRTY WORK IF THEY CAN HELP IT.
...ZOLA.
IT'S MY FAULT.
I KNEW THERE WERE RISKS IN SENDING YOU TO PARIS.
THEY'VE OBVIOUSLY BEEN PLANNING THIS FOR YEARS.
LONGER, ACTUALLY.
LONGER.
BUT—DuPREE WAS IN PARIS TOO! SHE WAS CERTAINLY WITH STURMVORAUS A LOT MORE THAN I EVER WAS.
YOU SAID SHE WAS CLEAN! IF THEY KNEW ABOUT ME—WHY DIDN'T THEY GET HER TOO?
IT WOULD HAVE BEEN EASY!
AN EXCELLENT QUESTION. SHE MIGHT HAVE VALUABLE INFORMATION—IF SHE LIVES.
IF SHE LIVES?
WHAT—
SHE BROUGHT
COLLAPSED.
SHE APPEARS TO HAVE BEEN POISONED.

POISONED?! NO! NOTHING IN THAT FORMULA SHOULD HAVE DONE THAT...
AND...AND EVEN IF STURMVORAUS' PEOPLE DID...DO SOMETHING TO ME,
I CAN'T BELIEVE THAT AGATHA—
SON! LISTEN TO YOURSELF!
I UNDERSTAND. YOU THINK YOU LOVE THIS GIRL.
AND I UNDERSTAND THAT YOU CAN'T HELP IT.
BUT SHE IS MORE A CHILD OF THE MONGFISH FAMILY THAN A HETERODYNE.
ALTHOUGH, LOOKING AT THE VAST BULK OF THEIR HISTORY, THE HETERODYNES AREN'T ANY BETTER, REALLY...
ACTUALLY, THEY'RE FAR, FAR WORSE.
BUT SHE IS HER MOTHER'S DAUGHTER, AND WITH THAT FAMILY,
YOU CAN BELIEVE NOTHING!
BUT IT'S ABSURD TO THINK SHE COULD HAVE PLANNED ALL THIS!
SHE WAS BROUGHT HERE BY MISTAKE!
WE BROUGHT HER HERE!
SHE WAS UNCONSCIOUS!
SHE DIDN'T ASK TO COME HERE!
SHE DIDN'T ASK US TO DO ANYTHING!
AND YET, HERE SHE WAS.
ON BOARD THE CASTLE.
IN YOUR LAB.
A VERY UNLIKELY COINCIDENCE—
AND I MISTRUST COINCIDENCES.
NOW. ALL OF EUROPA IS IN DANGER.
WE WILL TALK MORE WHEN I RETURN.

MEANWHILE, IN MECHANICSBURG—
MISS BAUMHUND, YOU HAVE AN UNFORTUNATE AURA OF FAILURE ABOUT YOUR PERSON.
THAT'S BECAUSE WE'VE FAILED, PROFESSOR.
AS FAR AS I CAN TELL, WE'RE THE LAST HOSTILE FORCE INSIDE MECHANICSBURG.
THAT WAS NOT THE PLAN, MISS BAUMHUND.
OLD KLAUS IS DEAD... OR AT LEAST WOUNDED...
TWENTY HETERODYNE IMPOSTERS ARE KILLING EACH OTHER INSIDE THE CASTLE,
AND THE HEIR TO THE EMPIRE HAS RUN OFF WITH THE STORM KING!
EVERYWHERE THERE IS CHAOS!
UM, WE DON'T KNOW THAT THE BARON IS DEAD...
IRRELEVANT! THIS TOWN IS RIPE FOR THE PLUCKING!
EXCEPT THAT THEY'VE BEATEN EVERYONE ELSE...
HA HA! BUT NOT US!
...AND DO YOU KNOW WHY?!
BECAUSE WE'VE BEEN HIDING IN A CELLAR.
BIDING OUR TIME!
—OR MAYBE BECAUSE THEY'VE CRUSHED YOUR "DOOM SQUIRRELS?"
THOSE TRAITOROUS SQUIRRELS LACKED THE WILL TO SERVE ME!
AH, BUT NOW...
NOW THE TOWN THINKS ITSELF SAFE!
IF WE ATTACK NOW-
THEY WILL BE COMPLETELY DEMORALIZED!
MUHAHAHAHA!
PROFESSOR, I REALLY DON'T THINK—
AND DON'T I KNOW IT-YOU'RE THE MOST TROUBLESOME GRAD STUDENT I'VE EVER HAD THE MISFORTUNE OF-AHA!
AHA?
THE FINAL TOUCH!
A CHARMING PAIR OF INNOCENT HOSTAGES!

SOON—

WELL, THE FIREFIGHTER CLANKS WERE BEING USED FOR *DEFENSE*—

SO WE JUST JURY-RIGGED A BUNCH OF SOLDIER CLANKS FOR A BUCKET BRIGADE...

PLEASE! WE *SURRENDER!*

JUST SEND SOMEONE TO HELP MY MEN BACK ON THAT ISLAND!

WHEN... WHEN THOSE LITTLE THINGS WENT FOR THEIR *FEET*—

THE FUTURE OF MECHANICSBURG IS SPOILED ROTTEN!

GREAT GREAT GREAT GRANDPA...

SPOILED ROTTEN I TELL YOU!!

...BUT SAFE.

WE...WE SEEK ASYLUM.

NOT EAT MANFLESH.

...SHOULD MENTION THAT DR. THMIZ ACTUALLY MADE FROM RECONSTITUTED SOY PRODUCTS.

TRAITOROUS SCUM!

I AM YOUR CREATOR!

AAAH! YOU *SWORE* YOU'D *NEVER TELL!*

WE HAVE ENOUGH FOOD STORES TO SURVIVE A TWO YEAR SIEGE,

BUT WE'RE ALREADY RUNNING SHORT OF *BUILDING* SUPPLIES.

WHEN *WINTER* COMES—

WULFENBACH FORCES HAVE CLEARED THE SKY.

ON ONE HAND, THIS IS *GOOD*, BUT IT ALSO MEANS THEY'VE EFFECTIVELY *SEALED US OFF*.

Soarece
...WHAT? I'M *WORKING,* OF COURSE.
OH! ZEETHA!

YOU MADE IT!
BUT OF COURSE!

—AND SO DID YOU! GOOD WORK—I KNEW YOU HAD IT IN YOU!
WELL, I HOPE SO...
BUT ANOTHER ATTACK COULD HIT US ANY MINUTE, AND WE'RE NOT READY!

AH, NOW, THAT IS WHAT I WANT TO TALK TO YOU ABOUT.
COME WITH ME!

WHAT? WHERE ARE WE GOING?
SOMEWHERE PRIVATE. YOU ARE IN SERIOUS NEED OF SOME PRINCESS LESSONS.

PRIN—WHAT?! NOW?!
YES. NOW. IT'S IMPORTANT.
YOU'RE THE NEW RULER OF MECHANICSBURG.
YOU NEED TO ACT LIKE IT.

WELL, MAYBE IF WE GET THROUGH ALL THIS, SURE—
BUT RIGHT NOW—

FIRST LESSON. EVERY PRINCESS NEEDS A BATTLE AXE.
HERE.
USE THIS ONE UNTIL WE FIND SOMETHING MORE IMPRESSIVE.

AH. THAT KIND OF PRINCESS.
COME ON. I SAW SOME ARMOR IN A BURNING MUSEUM THAT'S TO DIE FOR.

BUT I REALLY SHOULD GET BACK.
I WAS *WORKING.*
LIKE A MECHANIC.
BUT I *AM* A—
NOT ANY MORE.
"THEY SAY MY *MOTHER* USED TO DO THIS.
SHE WOULD TRY TO KILL EVERY FAFFLENARG BEAST *HERSELF.*"
"BUT SHE HAS AN *ARMY.*
SHE'S A *WAR QUEEN.*"
YOU ARE A WAR QUEEN.
AND YOU'VE GOT ME AND YOUR BOYS AND KROSP AND A *WHOLE TOWN* THAT WANTS YOU TO SUCCEED.
YOU NEED TO REMEMBER THAT, AND BE A *LEADER.*
WELL, OF *COURSE,* BUT...
BUT... I *LIKE* BUILDING STUFF.
I KNOW. AND WHEN YOU HAVE A MONTH—*HA*— EVEN A WEEK,
YOU CAN REBUILD THE WHOLE TOWN.
DO...DO YOU THINK THEY'LL *LET* ME?
THE POINT IS THAT *NOW* IS *NOT THE TIME!*
LET THE MECHANICS FIX THE CLANKS.
THERE ARE *HUNDREDS* OF
...BUT THERE'S ONLY ONE HETERODYNE—
AND THAT'S *YOU.*

SO. WHAT'S THE SITUATION?
WELL, I'M PRETTY SURE GIL GOT THROUGH.
THE WULFENBACH TROOPS HAVE PULLED BACK, AND THEY'VE STARTED HELPING US.
SPØNK
HMM...WELL, THAT'S GOOD—OOH, OOH, TRY THIS!
IF IT FITS, WE'LL ACCESSORIZE!
I DON'T THINK IT'S MY COLOR.
DOES THIS MAKE MY CHEST LOOK TOO BIG?
NO.
DRAT. BUT...YOU HAVEN'T HEARD FROM HIM?
NO, NOTHING.
HUH. I DON'T LIKE THAT.
I KNOW. KROSP SAYS THAT NO MATTER WHAT, REGAINING CONTROL OF THE EMPIRE WILL BE THEIR PRIORITY.
SURE. MECHANICSBURG IS SEALED. YOU'RE NOT GOING ANYWHERE.
UGH. ESPECIALLY IN THAT.
WHAT? I THOUGHT IT LOOKED DANGEROUS...
ONLY TO YOU.
THE EMPIRE IS ALSO ISOLATING YOU.
AH. YOU MEAN, WE'LL HAVE NO ALLIES.
RIGHT. HOW'S THE CASTLE?
AFTER THE BELL RANG, IT WENT ALMOST COMPLETELY DEAD.
WHAT ABOUT THIS?
NO WAY—CAN'T EVEN TELL YOU'RE A GIRL.
...NOW ALL IT DOES IS REQUEST A SPARK AND TELL THE TIME.
—REQUEST A SPARK? WHAT DOES IT WANT YOU TO DO NOW?
THE SAME THING EVERYONE ELSE EXPECTS ME TO DO, I SUPPOSE.
SAVE THE DAY.
...WELL, AT LEAST YOU'LL BE DRESSED FOR IT.

HY TINK DEY HAZ DONE SUMTING TO DER BEER VILE VE VAS GONE.
HO—HYU SOUND LIKE MY OL' POPPA...
"DEY CHUST AIN'T USIN' DE RIGHT KIND OV BLOOD IN DE BLOOD SAUSAGES DESE DAYS, BLAH BLAH BLAH."
HOY, HYU!
MAMMA! HULLO, DERE!
VERE IZ OUR GURL? SHE IN DERE?
HO, YEZ. IS VE UNDER ATTACK?
NOT YET, BUT—
DEN VE AIN'T LETTIN' HYU IN.
VOT?!
LEAF HER ALONE FOR A LEEDLE BIT.
SHE'S IN DERE HAFFING SUM GURL TOK VIT HER FRIEND.
SHE VAS NOT BORN UND RAISED AS A DAUGHTER OV DE HETERODYNES.
VOT SHE IZ DOINK NOW—BECOMING DE HETERODYNE—
IZ A LEEDLE LIKE VEN VUN BECOMES A JÄGER, HY TINK.
EVEN FOR A SCHMOT GURL LIKE HER, IZ BOUND TO BE A LEEDLE HARD.
SHE VILL BE RANTING UND FROTHING UND GOIN' ALL KREZY LIKE SOON ENUFF.
PAH!
HY VANTS TO SEE HER NOW!
HOY!
LATER.
VOT IZ DIS?!
HY IZ A GENERAL!
HO, HO! BUT HY VAS DETATCHED!
HY IZ A VILD JÄGER!
VORKING ON DOT SALUTING
MAXIM, AM I GUN REGRET TIPPING BECK MY HAT?
BORED DID HYU SAY HYU VOS?

WHAT'S GOING ON— MAMMA!
OH, THIS IS PERFECT! YOU'VE GOT TO COME UP HERE AND SEE THIS!
OH, HI, GUYS!
HELLO, MIZ ZEETHA.
vell, hy guess hyu kin go in now.
HYU IZ GOOT BOYZ.
HYU GO AHEAD AND KEEP ON LOOKINK AFTER HER...
BUT DUN' DO NOTTINK TOO SCHTUPID, HOKAY?
—AND SPEAKINK OV SCHTUPID—
VOT IZ HYU DOINK OUT OV BED?!
HYU GOTS A WHOLE BUNCH OV HEALINK TO DO, AND DUN HYU FORGET IT!
WELCOME TOURS HALF
YEEK!
NO FEAR OF THAT, I PROMISE.
BUT AGATHA NEEDS ME, AND YOU PATCHED ME UP WELL ENOUGH THAT I CAN AT LEAST GIVE HER ADVICE.
ANYWAY, THAT HIGGS ALREADY MADE ME PROMISE TO TAKE IT SLOW.
HE EVEN HID MY SWORDS.
...I FEEL NAKED.
HO HO! DOT BOY! ALVAYS VIT DE TRICKS!
YOU KNOW HIM WELL, THEN?
HO, YEZ INDEED!
COULD YOU...TELL ME ABOUT HIM?
HO. NO VAY, KIDDO.
VEN HE VANTS TO, HE'LL DO DOT HIMSELF.

UM...MAMMA? ARE YOU ALL RIGHT?
ONLY, THE LAST TIME I SAW PEOPLE CHANGING COLOR LIKE THAT,
EVERYBODY HAD TO GO TO AN AWFUL LOT OF TROUBLE TO MAKE SURE THEY DIDN'T BURST INTO FLAMES.
hee hee! DUN VORRY, SVEETIE. HY IZ FINE! BETTER DEN FINE!
TRYINK TO...BECOME JÄGERS...MOST PIPPLE JUST DIE—
BUT DE VUNS VOT LIVE GETS ALL KINDS OV GOODIES!
SOME GETS DE HORNS, OR DE TAILS—
OR DE GREAT BEEG TUSKS—RRROWR!
ME, HY GOTS DE FUN COLOR CHANGE-Y HEPIDERMOOSE!
HY VOS VERRA GOOT VEN DE HETERODYNES VERE GONE—
HY STAYED ALL SCHNEAKY-LIKE DE WHOLE TIME!
LIKE DIS. SEE?
IZ ZO NIZE TO RELAX UND MEK VIT DE PRETTY COLORS AGAIN—HYU VOULD NOT BELIEVE—
YEEK!
HY DIDN'T KNOW DEY KEPT DOT TING!
STILL, HY GOTS TO ADMIT DOT VOS SOME PARTY...
...ahem. RIGHT. BUSINESS. VERE IZ DE MISTRESS?
HY GOTS TO TALK TO HER ABOUT DOT STORM KING OF HERS.
TARVEK? YEAH, WHERE IS HE?
WE COULD'VE REALLY USED HIS HELP HERE!
GOTT'S LEEDLE FEESH IN TROUSERS!

ELSEWHERE—
—WHY, EVEN AS MY SPUNKY GIRL ASSISTANT, SHE—
SAY, ARE YOU ALL RIGHT?
OH, NO, IT'S NOTHING... PLEASE DO CONTINUE.
WELL, HERR TRYGGVASSEN, WE WOULD BE VERY HONORED IF YOU WERE TO STAY AND HELP US OUT!
BUT OF COURSE!
AS I WAS SAYING, WITH PROPER TRAINING, YOUR NEW HETERODYNE WILL MAKE A SPLENDID HERO!
I'LL NEED TO SHOW HER THE ROPES A BIT LONGER, OF COURSE, BUT—
ugh. I CAN'T LISTEN TO ANY MORE OF THIS.
—AND YES, VIOLETTA, I KNOW YOU'RE THERE.
ER...
WHY AREN'T YOU WITH AGATHA?
I WAS. SHE SENT ME TO LOOK FOR YOU.
SHE DID?
WHATEVER FOR?
ER... WELL...
WHAT?
WELL—
AT FIRST SHE THOUGHT MAYBE YOU'D RUN OFF BECAUSE OF WULFENBACH—
AND I SAID THAT THERE WAS NO WAY A WEASEL LIKE YOU WOULD GIVE UP THAT EASILY—
AND THEN SHE SAID IN THAT CASE, IF YOU WERE GONE, IT MUST MEAN YOU'D RUN INTO SOMETHING EITHER REALLY IMPORTANT OR REALLY DANGEROUS—
BECAUSE, UM, SHE SAID: "IF HE'S THAT MUCH OF A WEASEL,"
ER..."THEN HE'D KNOW THAT HIS BEST ADVANTAGE LIES IN STICKING CLOSE TO ME."
AGATHA SAID THAT?
UM—YEAH. SORRY.
NO, NO! THIS IS MARVELOUS! SHE MIGHT BE BETTER AT THIS THAN I'D HOPED!

SHE'LL BE *FANTASTIC,* ASSUMING SHE *LIVES.*
LET'S *GO* ALREADY.
OH, SURE. GREAT IDEA. I HADN'T THOUGHT OF *THAT.*

WHAT— YOU'RE TELLING ME YOU CAN'T GET AWAY FROM A BUNCH OF *TOWN GUARDS?*
FINE. LET'S TRY A "DOWN AND UP."
THAT MIGHT WORK.
SERIOUSLY—?
GO!

IF THIS IS SOME KIND OF *JOKE—*
JUST *RUN!*
HEY! GET BACK HERE!

THERE! *THIS* SHOULD—
KEEP GOING!

SPLISH
SPLISH SPLISH
SPLISH SPLISH SPLISH

BLANG!
THUP
THUP
THUP

ROOF
WAS THERE A *POINT* TO ALL THIS?
UM

NOW WHERE ARE YOU GOING? WE STILL HAVE TO *FIND AGATHA!*
AH! AND I SEE YOU'VE FOUND ME *ANOTHER ASSISTANT!*

WHAT?! BUT— *HOW?!*
THIS IS WHY HE'S A *HERO.*
HE'S VERY, *VERY* GOOD AT THIS.

BUT—LADY HETERODYNE TOLD ME TO BRING HIM BACK RIGHT AWAY!
AH, SHE JUST DIDN'T KNOW THAT OTHAR TRYGGVASSEN WAS HERE!
YOU TWO CAN JUST RELAX AND LET ME HANDLE EVERYTHING!
LET ME GO, YOU CRETIN! I HAVE TO GET TO HER QUICKLY!
ACTUALLY, I'M FROM NORWAY...
I HAVE IMPORTANT MILITARY INFORMATION! WE'LL NEED TO RE-THINK ALL OF OUR DEFENSES!
IF ANY OF US ARE GOING TO GET THROUGH THIS ALIVE—
O-HO! VOT KIND OV MILITARY INFORMATION HYU GOTS, HEY?
NO. IT SHOULDN'T BE SPREAD AROUND. I NEED TO TELL AGATHA.
HMM. HY SEE...
HOKAY, HY TAKE DIS GUY VIT ME.
ARE YOU SURE, JORGI? HE'S—
heh. HY KNOWS WHO HE IZ!
YOU DO?
HO, YEZ!
BUT...WHAT ABOUT VIOLETTA?
OH, VELL, HY DUNNO...
YOU'D BETTER TAKE ME, YOU SLUG!
MY LADY NEEDS YOU—
AND SINCE I'M STILL NOT CONVINCED YOU CAN USE A FORK PROPERLY,
I WANT YOU WHERE I CAN SEE YOU!
SO, I SHOULD MENTION THAT VIOLETTA HERE IS A SMOKE KNIGHT.
GOODNESS! REALLY?
OH, YES...AND SHE'LL DENY IT, BUT SHE'S A HUGE FAN.
A SMOKE KNIGHT, YOU SAY.
hmm. IN THAT CASE, SHE MIGHT EVEN LAST THROUGH THE SUMMER!
I... WHAT?
YOU...
TA! KEEP HIM OUT OF TROUBLE, LITTLE COUSIN!
I WILL HUNT YOU DOWN, FLAY YOU, AND WEAR YOU AS A HAT!
AND SHE'S CERTAINLY GOT THE SPUNKY PART DOWN!

HYU GOTS TO EXCUSE DER TOWN COUNCIL—
DE OLD GUYS HAVE BEEN TRAPPING VIT DE TOURISTS TOO LONG—
AN' DE YOUNG GUYS IZ SCHTILL *FIGURIN' TINGS OUT.*
MARKYYS BRAND SNAILS "SLOW AND SWEET"
GREEN DEVILS ARE IN!
DEY'S STILL TINKING LIKE A BUNCH OV SOFT *TOWNIES.*
NOT DAT DOTS A *BAD* TING—
SOMEBODY GOTS TO DO DE *RUNNING UND SCREAMING...*
EH, BUT DIS IZ MECHANICSBURG, UND DEY'S IT'S PIPPLE. DEY'LL VAKE OP SOON ENUFF—
UND DEN, *VATCH OUT!*
BUT DOT VILL TEK SOME TIME. UND SINCE DER *STORM KING* VANTS TO MAKE VIT DER MILITARY TALK *NOW*—
PRIVATE PARTY
SHHH! QUIET! THAT'S STILL A SECRET!
VOT? OH, DUN VORRY, DESE GUYS DUN HOLD GRUDGES ABOUT *DOT* OLD SCTUFF.
HIF HYU DUN LEARN HOW TO LET SCHTUFF LIKE *DOT* GO—
HYU DUN LAST LONG ENUF TO BECOME A *GENERAL.*

AH— WE MEET AGAIN?
IT'S A *RULE,* OKAY?
WHEN YOU SIT AT THE GENERALS' TABLE, YOU'VE GOT TO HAVE A *HAT.*
...*HE* DOESN'T HAVE A HAT.
OH DEARIE ME— DID I FORGETS MINE *HAT?*
HA HA HA HA HA HA HA HA HEE HA HA HEE HEE
HOOHO
HA HA HA HEE HEE HEE
WHAT THE— WE'RE ABOUT TO BE UNDER ATTACK AND YOU GUYS ARE *JOKING AROUND?!*
DON'T BLAME THEM.
THEY'RE *WORRIED.*
WORRIED?
BY TRADITION, THE NEW HETERODYNE SHOULD BE GREETED BY *ALL* THE GENERALS.
GENERAL ØSK DIED FIGHTING THE POLAR LORDS' DOOM WYRM LAST YEAR.
THAT LEAVES *SEVEN.*
FOUR ARE HERE—
SO WHERE ARE THE OTHERS?
COULD THERE BE... *DISSENSION* HERE?
WAIT— *SEVEN?* I HEARD *SIX.*
...
HOKAY.
NO FONNY HAT FOR *HYU.*
COME *TALK* VIT US.

HYU IZ RIGHT. DERE IZ SEVEN OV US NOW.
NOT MANY PIPPLE KNOWS DOT.
GENERAL GKIKA IZ VIT DE LADY HETERODYNE.
SHE VILL BRING HER HERE SOON.
GENERAL ZADIPOK SHOULD BE HERE BY NOW—
BUT VE HAFF NOT HEARD FROM HIM.
IT IZ, AS HYU SAY, VORRYING.
UND DE SEVENTH, VELL, HE IZ A TRICKY VUN.
HE IZ...DE KEEPER OV MANY SECRET TINGS.
...AND WHY ISN'T HE HERE?
DE ODDER INSIDE DE LADY.
"THE OTHER—" YOU KNOW ABOUT THAT?
HEH. INDEED VE DOES.
AND AS LONG AS DOT BAD GURL IZ IN DE LADY'S HEAD,
HE VILL REMAIN IN DE SHADOWS.
OF COURSE. BUT...
WELL...LET HIM KNOW THAT HE MAY NOT HAVE TO STAY THERE.
I'VE STUDIED HER METHODS, AND I BELIEVE I CAN GET LUCREZIA OUT OF AGATHA'S HEAD FOR GOOD.
OH-HO. DOT IZ GOOT NEWS.
AH. AND DEN HYU CAN GETS TO DE KEESING, YEZ?
WELL, I'M CERTAINLY NOT GOING TO DO IT BEFORE—
heh heh heh. HEY, BOYZ—DOT WULFENBACH KEED GOTS HIM A RIVAL!
WAIT! NO! I DIDN'T— THAT IS—
DIS IZ GUN BE FUN!
ARE THEY ALWAYS LIKE THIS?
I'M GUESSING— YES.
ahem. ANYWAY, AGATHA'S GOT LUCREZIA UNDER CONTROL, FOR NOW.
WE HAVE A BIGGER, MORE IMMEDIATE PROBLEM.
THE BARON—

BOOM BOOM BOOM
VOT IZ DIS NOW?!
HOY! DEY'S NOT ATTACKING US—DEY'S SHOOTINK AT VUN OV DERE OWN SHIPS!
BOOM BOOM
BOOM
NO! I THOUGHT THEY COULD GET THROUGH IF—
...VELL, DOT KEN'T BE GOOT.
OOH.
DEY GOTS IT, TOO.
DUN HYU KNOW NOTTINK? DOT VAS A DELIBERATE FORCED LANDINK!
IZ HYU KREZY? DEY COULD'VE BEEN KILT!
DEY VAS ALREADY GETTINK SHOT AT!
DER NORTH SIDE OV TOWN VAS ALREADY PRETTY MESSED OP—HEY! DER ODDER SHIPS IS LOWERING LINES!
HUH. DEY'S SENDING IN TROOPS.
AWWW— VY DUN IT BLOW OP?
'COS DOT ONLY HOPPENS IN DOSE CHEAP NOVELS, HYU OLD FOOL.
tsk. DEY'S HUNTINK DERE OWN PIPPLE.
WHO CARES? DEY'S LANDING DOSE TROOPS IN OUR TOWN!
WE'VE GOT TO HURRY! I NEED THE PEOPLE FROM THAT SHIP ALIVE!
I SINCERELY HOPE YOU GENTLEMEN FIGHT AS WELL AS YOU DRESS.
US?
FIGHT?
VELL...
VOT? DIS OLD TING?

ALL CIVILIANS ARE TO LEAVE THE AREA.
ANYONE WHO REMAINS WILL BE *SHOT*.
TUKKEN
REMEMBER— *NO ONE* LEAVES THAT SHIP *ALIVE*.
SHINGG
AAAAAAAAAAH!!
HOY! DOES DOT *COUNT?*
DOES KILLINK DEM VEN DEY IZ *IN DE AIR* COUNT?
KILLINK HYU ENEMIES *ALWAYS* COUNTS.

STAND DOWN, GENERAL!
WE'RE NOT HERE TO FIGHT WITH YOU, BUT IF YOU INTERFERE, OUR GUNNER CLANKS—
OH, DEZE TINGS? SORRY ABOUT DOT, BOYZ, DEY FALLS RIGHT OVER!
DEY VOS INVADING OUR TOWN, HYU KNOW...
VE KENT HAFF DOT!
NOW, HOW BOUTS HYU SURRENDER LIKE GENTLEMEN?
OH! NO—VAIT! EVEN BETTER! HY DUELS HYU CHAMPION!
THIS ISN'T SOME GAME!
THE PEOPLE IN THAT AIRSHIP ARE DANGEROUS TRAITORS!
WE HAVE DIRECT ORDERS FROM THE BARON TO WIPE THEM OUT.
SORRY, BUT VE GOTS A GUY HERE WHO VANTS DEM ALIVE.
...UND VOT'S VIT DE LEEDLE SWORDS, HEY?
HYU MAKING FUN OV ME OR SOMETING?
DON'T WORRY, THERE'S ENOUGH TOXIN HERE TO TAKE DOWN EVEN A BEHEMOTH LIKE YOU.
ENOUGH.
MEN! KILL THEM ALL.
FEH. DIZ HARDLY SEEMS FAIR...
C'EST LA GUERRE, GENERAL.
Snak!
AHH!
Flick!
URK!
HY DUN MEAN FOR ME.
EEE!
AIEE!
GAKK!
Flick! Flick! Flick! Flicketty Flick!
SO...HY S'POSE HYU TINK DOT COUNTS TOO? USING DERE OWN WEAPONS?
OV CAUZE! DE VEAPONS DUN CARE!

SIR! THEY'RE WIPING US OUT!
RIGHT. THE BARON CAN'T SAY WE DIDN'T *TRY*—
SO *NOW* WE'LL DO THIS *MY WAY*.
DISENGAGE!
BUT—OUR *ORDERS*...
WE'LL JUST *GAS* THE WHOLE AREA AND BURN IT DOWN *FROM THE AIR*.
IT'S WHAT WE *SHOULD HAVE DONE* IN THE *FIRST PLACE*.
HO! NOW HYU GUYS IZ JUST *ASKING* FOR IT.

WE'RE *NOT* GOING TO FIGHT *YOU*, GARGANTUA.
WE'RE *DONE HERE*.
TOO BAD YOU DIDN'T STICK WITH *OUR SIDE*—
NOW YOU'LL BURN WITH THE REST OF THE FROTHING LOONIES AND SHORT-CHANGE ARTISTS IN THIS *BACKWATER DUMP!*
RIP!
CRAK

UND KILLINK DEM VEN DEY'S *RUNNING AVAY*, DIS *ALSO COUNTS?*
...
VOT IN DE DUMBOOZLE IZ
VIT HYU?

VELL...
HY JUST DUN VANT HYU GUYZ SAYING I VOS *CHEATING*.
...*HOW* SO?
...USING DEY OWN VEAPONS...
VILE DEY IZ *IN DE AIR*—
VOWM!
VOWM!
BOOM!
BEFORE DEY KEN GETS TO DER *RUNNING AVAY?*
SO ALL DOT *COUNTS?*
DEN HY *VIN*.
hmf. IZ *STILL CHEATING*.
BUT IN DER *GOOT* VAY!

CLEP CLEP CLEP
VERRA NIZE!
CLEP CLEP CLEP
YAH! BEAUTIFULLY DONE!
OH. UH... WOW.
UM, SO...
SO IT'LL PROBABLY TAKE AT LEAST A FEW MINUTES FOR THEM TO SEND SOMETHING ELSE...
BUT I'M WORRIED. WHY HASN'T ANYONE LEFT THE AIRSHIP?
HEH. VOULD HYU?
VE IZ OUT HERE!
NO. SOMETHING'S WRONG.
LET'S GO!
ZO VOTS DE BEEG DEAL VIT DESE GUYS, ANYVAY?
AS FAR AS THE EMPIRE IS CONCERNED, THEY'RE SOME OF THE MOST DANGEROUS PEOPLE ALIVE.
HETERODYNE MUSEUM of ARMOR
HO! JUST LIKE US! DEY VILL FIT RIGHT IN DEN, YAH?
MECHANICSBURG IS GOOT PLACE FOR DANGEROUS PIPPLE!
YES... AND THE EMPIRE... LUCREZIA... KNOWS THAT.
VE SHOULD CALL DE VELCOME VAGON! DEY GOTS DEEZ GREAT LEEDLE SAMMICHES AND CUTE GURLS IN HAZ-MAT SUITS!
STILL, IT'S NOT LIKE THEY REALLY NEED ANOTHER REASON TO REDUCE THIS WHOLE TOWN TO A SMOKING CRATER...
VAITAMINUTE! DOSE GUYS? DEY IZ VAT EFFERYVUN IS VORRIED ABOUT?

PRINCE STURMVORAUS!
YOU WERE *RIGHT!*
YOU WERE RIGHT ABOUT *EVERYTHING!*
AND IT'S EVEN *WORSE* THAN WE *THOUGHT—*
YES, YES, I KNOW.
BUT WHAT'S WRONG HERE?
THE WASP EATERS ARE STILL INSIDE.
WE'RE TRYING TO GET TO THEM NOW, BUT WE'RE HAVING TROUBLE GETTING CLOSE.
OH? WHY?
SOMETHING GOT BROKEN WHEN WE CRASHED...
SEVERAL OF OUR PEOPLE ARE *DEAD*...INCLUDING DOCTOR BREN.
BREN? *DEAD?*
THEN IF WE LOSE THE WASP EATERS, THIS WILL *ALL* HAVE BEEN *POINTLESS!*
JÄGERS! *FOLLOW ME!*

BOOM!
SHREEEEEEE!
SHREEEK!
SHREEEEEEEEEEEE!
SCREE!
WHOA!
NO!
HEY, HYU BETTER STAY HERE, YAH?
ONLY, HYU REGULAR PIPPLE IZ KINDA FRAGILE—
UND I DUNNO IF DE LADY VOULD LIKE IT TOO MUCH IF VE GOTS HYU BROKEN...
ENOUGH!
THE IMPORTANCE OF THESE CREATURES CANNOT BE OVERESTIMATED!
YOU WILL FOLLOW ME AND DO AS I SAY, OR I WILL HAVE YOU ALL FLAYED, ROASTED ALIVE, AND TURNED INTO STOATS!
HEY, WHO'S HE TINK HE IZ, GIVINK US ORDERS LIKE DOT?
HEH. VE'S FOLLOWING, AIN'T VE?
YAH, NO KIDDING! DOT VUN GOTS DE GREAT RANTING VOICE!
NO VUNDER DE LADY LIKE HIM, HEY?
HE MUST BE VUN HECKUVA DEMON VIT DE SVEET TOK!
I DUNNO, DOT ODDER VUN GOTS A MIGHTY NIZE HAT...

SO, THROUGH HERE, THERE'S—
JÄGERS!
LET'S GO!
CRUNK!
HOY!
HY SHOULD VARN HYU—
NOT ALL OV OUR BOYZ GUN PUT OP VIT HYU BOSSINK US AROUND LIKE—
SCREEEEEEEK!
JORGI! VOT HYU DOING?!
HYU IZ MISSING VUN GREAT FIGHT!
...HOKAY, BOSS. HYU VIN DIS VUN.
COMINK!
tsk. I KNEW THAT THING WOULD GET LOOSE...
I DON'T KNOW WHY BREN EVEN KEPT IT...

SHREEEEEEE!
SMAK!
THOK!
WOOHOO!
OKAY. LET'S GET THE WASP EATERS *OUT* OF HERE.
RIGHT. THIS WAY—
OH, *NO.*
I'M SORRY, CAPTAIN!
I'M SO SORRY—
WE'VE LOST *SO MANY OF THEM!*
WEASEL CHOW
WHAT— NO—NEVER MIND!
COLLECT THE REST—
AAH! CAPTAIN!
...

HIVE WARRIORS!
MISS, YOU'VE GOT TO RUN!

MOVE!
OOF

CHUT!

POF!

ER...
PROTECTING PEOPLE FROM THEM IS MY JOB.
AH—I'M... I'M SORRY, YOU JUST SEEMED RATHER... DISTRAUGHT—

OF COURSE I'M DISTRAUGHT!
POF!
THEY HURT MY WEASELS!

RIGHT. LET'S GET AS MANY CAGES AS WE CAN CARRY.
OH, ALL WE HAVE TO DO IS *OPEN* THEM.
LUGGING ALL THE CAGES WOULD TAKE TOO LONG, AND WE HAVE TO HURRY. YOU NEVER KNOW WHAT *ELSE* DOCTOR BREN WAS KEEPING IN HIS LAB.
DON'T WORRY, THESE LITTLE GUYS ARE SMART ENOUGH TO FOLLOW US OUT.
"WHAT *ELSE* HE MIGHT HAVE HAD—?"
WHAT ELSE *MIGHT* HE HAVE HAD?!
WELL, THERE SHOULD BE AT LEAST TWO MORE OF THOSE WARRIORS, SO BE CAREFUL.
NO—WAIT—YOU *BROUGHT* THEM HERE?
OF COURSE. OUR JOB IS TO DETECT AND DESTROY THEM.
THAT INCLUDES *STUDYING* THEM.
WE ALSO USE THEM TO TRAIN THE WASP EATERS.
THAT... MAKES SENSE...
UM, YOU DON'T HAVE ANY ACTUAL *ENSLAVERS* HERE, DO YOU?
OF *COURSE* NOT. NOT LIVE ONES, ANYWAY.
I'M RELIEVED. SURPRISED, BUT RELIEVED.
YEAH, THEY DON'T LAST LONG OUTSIDE THEIR ENGINES.
AH. OF COURSE.
COME ON OUT, SWEETIES!
LET'S GO!
HUH. I DIDN'T KNOW THEY WERE SO *TAME*.
OH, THEY'RE *NOT*.
THEY CAN BE QUITE VICIOUS WHEN THEY SENSE WASPS,
BUT MOSTLY, THEY JUST IGNORE PEOPLE. UNLESS...
sniff sniff
OH. ER...
UNLESS THEY *REALLY LIKE YOU!*
EEEEEEE.
... LUCKY ME.

FOOM!
FOOM!
WHOA! NOT GOOD!
BOOM!
YOU, THERE! WHAT ARE YOU DOING?
HURRY UP AND GET OUT!
BREN'S LAB! QUICKLY! WHICH WAY IS IT?
I'VE JUST COME FROM THERE!
IT'S FULL OF WULFENBACH STEALTH FIGHTERS!
THEY'RE KILLING EVERYTHING THEY SEE—
BUT DON'T WORRY—I MANAGED TO SET MOST OF THE EXPERIMENTS FREE BEFORE THEY GOT IN!
SO SOME OF THEM GOT THROUGH...AND WHY AM I NOT SURPRISED THAT THERE ARE EXPERIMENTS?
WELL, DUH.
...DID YOU GET BREN'S NOTES?
JEEZ, I WAS LUCKY TO GET OUT OF THERE ALIVE!
FINE. YOU TWO GET THE WASP EATERS OUT OF HERE.
THEY'RE OUR FIRST PRIORITY.
WAIT! WHERE ARE YOU GOING?
I WANT THOSE NOTES!
BUT...I DON'T EVEN KNOW IF BREN KEPT NOTES!
...AND THERE'S MONSTERS! AND CRAZY KILLERS!
YOU'VE GOT NOTHING!
NONSENSE!
I HAVE YOUR KNIFE AND YOUR GUN.
...
OH MAN, I'M GONNA HEAR ABOUT THAT.

OH, *PERFECT.*
WHICH ONE IS *BREN'S?*
I HOPE IT WASN'T *THAT* ONE...

HERE. THIS IS BREN'S OFFICE.
...AND HURRY UP—SOME OF THIS STUFF CAN BE *REALLY VOLATILE.*
AH! *THESE* LOOK RIGHT!
YES!
GOOD! IS THERE A BAG OR SOMETHING I CAN USE?
URGH!
I THINK YOU'LL BE NEEDING A *COFFIN.*
HEH. GOOD ONE. MAKE THAT *TWO!*

KILL HIM. GRAB THOSE NOTES.
FINISH THE GIRL.
YES SIR!
NO.
I THINK NOT.
WHAT THE— HE JUMPED INTO THE FIRE?!
WHY?! WE WERE GONNA KILL HIM JUST FINE!
URK.
SHUNK
YOU KNOW, I'M NOT REALLY MUCH FOR THE WHOLE "SCHOOL PRIDE" THING—
HA?
HRAAAAH!
BUT YOU CLODS AREN'T FIT TO SHINE A SMOKE KNIGHT'S KNIVES!
SNAP!
AH— YOU'RE STILL ALIVE. GOOD.
...
OF COURSE, THAT MEANS I'LL HAVE TO CARRY YOU...
dook!

...AND WE'D BETTER *MOVE*, TOO,
THAT FIRE'S SPREADING *FAST*.
DOOK!
I HOPE THEY GOT ALL THE WASP EATERS OUT...
PITY ABOUT THE SHIP...
AND ALL THE *EQUIPMENT*...
OOF. THIS GIRL IS HEAVIER THAN SHE LOOKS.
HMF. I *TOLD* YOU TO *GET OUT*.
I COULD HAVE FOUND BREN'S OFFICE WITHOUT HELP...
WELL...
PROBABLY...
WAR
tch. CRACK VESPIARY SQUAD—
ALL THAT TRAINING AND YOU GET STABBED BY *MORONS*.
WHAT GOOD DID IT DO YOU?
ACK!
POF!
OKAY...THE TRAINING *IS* IMPRESSIVE.
UGH. TOO *SLOW*.
SORRY, CAPTAIN—
TUMMY HURTS

OOF. WHAT I WOULDN'T GIVE FOR ANEVKA'S STRONG BOYS NOW...
HOY, DERE, BOSS!
A JÄGER! CLOSE ENOUGH!
WHOO! DOT VOS VUN KREZY VEASEL MONSTER HYU FIND FOR US, HYU BETCHA!
GOOT FUN, YAH!
AH, WHAT HAPPENED TO IT?
HEH. HY DUNNO. GRISHNARF UND SHADSNAF VOS CHASINK IT.
OH.
ZO— BEEG DATE?
HO HO. WE HAVE TO LEAVE. NOW.
CAN YOU HELP ME OUT, HERE?
NO.
OH, COME ON. PLEASE. I'LL GET A NOTE FROM AGATHA—
DOT REALLY VAS VUN KREZY VEASEL MONSTER TING.
HY GOTS BROKEN BONES IN DE SHOULDER UND BOTH LEGS.
WHAT?!
tch. DUN VORRY, VE HEALS FAST.
HOKAY, NOT DOT FAST.
HO, VELL. HYU BETTER GETS MOVIN', KEEDO.
HIF HYU VIN, HYU TREAT HER GOOT, HOKAY?
...UND DEN GRISHNARF SAID HYU IZ PROBABLY SUM KIND OV SCHNEAKY SCHNEAK,
BUT HY FIGURE HYU IS A GOOT GUY AFTER ALL, HEY?
SAY, HY DUN SUPPOSE HYU GOTS A SANDVICH ON HYU ENNYVERE...
STOP!
TALKING!

DUN FEEL BAD. HYU KEN GETS US ALL SANDVICHES YUNCE VE'S OUT OV HERE.
MUST.
LIVE.
TO.
KILL.
ZO, VOT'S DESE BOOKS, HEY?
IZ DEY IMPAWTENT?
PUT THAT DOWN, YOU ILLITERATE FOOL!
SHADDUP, SCHMOT GUY. HY KEN READ.
GOOD HEAVENS. REALLY?
SURE—BUT IF HYU TELLS DE ODDER GUYS, HY RIP HYU HEAD OFF!
AH, OF COURSE...
MINE POPPA VOS A BLACKSMITH, BUT HE VANTED TO BE A PHILOSOPHER.
HE EVEN MADE MINE SISTERS LEARN TO READ.
HE VAS BEEG INTO DUALITY UND DE POLITICS OF NON-BEINK AS RELATED TO PLATONIC REALITY.
...REALLY?
HO! TRICK QVESTION!
BUT, YOU JOINED—
HEY—HYU LEESEN TO A GUY LIKE DOT FOR FIFTEEN YEARS,
HYU VILL VANT TO BURN DOWN DE VORLD, TOO.
ARE...ARE ALL THE JÄGERS LIKE YOU?
NAH. MOST OV US JUST LIKES HITTIN' HYU GUYS.
UNLIKE YOU.
MEH, I LIKES IT, TOO. ZO, VOT'S IN HERE—?
OH. DE VEASEL TINGS. HUH.
SQUEE! DOOK! DOOK!
WHAT NOW?!
MORE JÄGERS?
ORPHANS?
JÄGER ORPHANS?
OH.
SKEEE!
NEEP!
NEEP?
HUH. DESE TINGS AIN'T SUPPOSED TO HAFF BABBIES...
LOOKS LIKE RIGHT NOW, DEY GOTS TO USE ALL DIS EQVIPMENT—
WHAT?
OH! HY RECOGNIZE DOT, HY BROKE DOT!
OOH, HY SEE. DIS GUY VOS VORKING ON IT—
DESE MUST BE SOME KIND OV NEW TYPE!

THOOM!
HEY, BOSS—
I HEAR IT. I HEAR IT.
EEF HYU LETS ME OFF HERE—
NO! WE'RE ALMOST OUT!
THOOM!
DOT DUN SOUND LIKE EXPLOSIONS...
YOU'RE AN EXPERT?
SURE, HYU BUST OP ENOUGH SCHTUFF, HYU LEARNS ALL KINDS OV TINGS.
VATEFFER DOT IZ, IT IZ A BIG VUN.
WRONG DIRECTION.
THAT GIANT WASP EATER?
MAYBE ANOTHER ONE?
HY SURE HOPES NOT.
DOT TING VOS KRENKY MEAN.
VOT HYU SCHMOT GUYS VANT SOMETING LIKE DOT FOR, ENNYVAY?
I...I DON'T KNOW.
THESE LITTLE ONES HERE ARE ALREADY GREAT AGAINST THE WASPS.
THEY'LL SNAP UP THE SWARMERS, AND MOB THE WARRIORS—
BUT THAT THING YOU GUYS WERE FIGHTING WAS BIG ENOUGH TO TAKE ON—
HHHHHHHHHHZZZZZZZZZZKKKREEE!
UH... A HIVE QUEEN?
SKREEEK!
SKEEE!
HO! EVERYTING MAKE VIT DE PERFECT SENSE NOW!

THIS IS RIDICULOUS!
HIVE QUEENS ARE SUPPOSED TO BE SESSILE!
SO—
NOT—
FAIR!
HEY! HY BET DIS BEEG VUN VOULD MAKE A NIZE BUG PIE!
VEN HYU IZ DONE VIT IT, KEN I HAFF A COUPLE OV DE LEGS?
HY IZ A GOOT COOK! HY GIVE HYU SOME UND HYU'LL SEE!
OOOH, HYU IZ ALMOST TO DE DOOR!
LOOK! IT'Z BEHIND DOT GIANT WALL OV FLAME OVER DERE!
YOU WEIGH LESS WHEN YOU'RE NOT TALKING!
VOT DE—
WHAT ARE YOU PEOPLE DOING?!
RUN!
SKEE!
WHOA! DOT TING IZ STILL COMINK AFTER US!
WHAT?! OH, COME ON! WHAT'S WRONG WITH THIS MONSTER?
SOME OF THOSE PEOPLE LOOK DELICIOUS!

HOO, IT DUN LOOK DOT BIG *INSIDE*...
THERE'S AN ALLEY AHEAD!
MAYBE THAT THING WILL BE *TOO BIG*...
HALT!
THIS ALLEY IS THE HEADQUARTERS OF THE GLORIOUS MECHANICSBURG CHILDREN'S CRUSADE, PEANUT MILITIA AND STINK-BOMBERS SECRET SOCIETY OF *JUSTICE!*
WHAT'S THE PASSWORD?
FINE! YOU GET THESE PEOPLE TO SAFETY!
VOT?!
YEEK!
FWUMP!
BACK OFF, MONSTER!
HRAAAAH!
OH... RIGHT...
THAT NEVER *DID* WORK...

GAAAAH!
ZZA-CRAK!
WHAT DO YOU THINK YOU'RE DOING?!
AH...

ARE YOU *LOOKING* FOR AN EXCUSE TO *DIE?!*
YOU *IDIOT!* I SHOULD JUST-
UGH. HOLD ON...
STUPID *LEVERS...*
UM... *WULFENBACH?* IS THAT—
YOU?
...*THERE.*

WHERE HAVE YOU BEEN?!
WHAT ARE WE SUPPOSED TO DO IF YOU GO AND GET YOURSELF KILLED?!
AGATHA!
I...
I...
UM...
WHAT... WHATEVER YOU WANT?

JUST A MINUTE. I'LL BE RIGHT DOWN.
CLUNK
CLAK
CLAK
CLAK
SO—ARE YOU HURT?
YOU LOOK AWFUL.
...YOU LOOK BEAUTIFUL.
WHAT?
UM...RIGHT. SURE. BECAUSE I ALWAYS LOOK STUNNING WHEN I'VE BEEN CRAWLING AROUND WORKING ON GREASY OLD MACHINERY AND...AND...
THAT'S RIGHT.
ALWAYS.

—SHE GOTS OL' VORTHANG'S SUNDAY BEST ARMOR *VORKING!*
YEZ...NOT EVEN HER *POPPA* COULD DO *DOT!*
ZO, DIS GUY SAVED JORGI, DID HE? *GOOOOT...*
THE BLADES WERE POISONED, BUT YOUR MISS VIOLETTA KNEW THE ANTIDOTE—
SO RUXALA WILL BE *FINE* ONCE SHE'S HAD TIME TO *HEAL.*
EXCELLENT! THAT'S MY *SPUNKY GIRL SIDEKICK!*
—AND *YOU,* SIR!
YOU DID A *FINE JOB* IN THERE!
YOU SHOW GREAT PROMISE INDEED!
WHY, AS MY *HAPLESS ARRRENTICE HERO,* YOU SHOULD—
BAF!
THAT'S THE *SECOND* THING I PROMISED MYSELF I'D DO IF I GOT OUT OF ALL THAT ALIVE.
FOUL!

...AND...AND HERE GOES THE OTHER.
AGATHA— I'VE JUST GOT TO SAY THIS PROPERLY ONCE, SO YOU KNOW.
AFTER THAT, I'LL SHUT UP ABOUT IT AND WE'LL GET BACK TO WORK—
SO LISTEN CAREFULLY.
WULFENBACH... HE LOVES YOU. HE REALLY DOES.
...AND YOU—WELL, I WAS READY TO GIVE UP ANY HOPE THAT YOU MIGHT EVER CARE FOR ME—
...BUT I LOVE YOU, TOO. FOR A THOUSAND REASONS.
...AND I'M NOT GIVING UP AFTER ALL.
IF GIL WINS YOUR HEART IN THE END, IT WON'T BE WITHOUT A FIGHT.
THERE. I SAID IT.
NOW, ARE THERE ANY MAPS OF THE CURRENT DEFENSES?
I'D REALLY LIKE A LOOK AT THEM IF I COULD.
ER...
...
AH, YES! UM...I'LL...I'LL TAKE YOU TO THEM.
...AND WHERE DID YOU FIND THAT AMAZING ANTIQUE BATTLE ARMOR?
IS THERE ANYTHING ELSE LIKE THAT LYING AROUND?
OH, ISN'T IT FANTASTIC?!
THERE'S NOTHING ELSE EXACTLY LIKE THAT, BUT THERE ARE HEAPS OF OTHER THINGS IN THERE!
HOO! DIS VUN FIGHTS DIRTY! WULFENBACH GOTS TROUBLE NOW, YAH?
THIRTY—IN GOLD—ON STURMVORAUS!
HEY KEED, GIMMEE VUN HUNENRT ON HER TAKINK BOTH UV DEM!
THAT'S THE DARK HORSE, GENERAL. ONE WILL GET YOU FIVE.
WHAT? YOU HAD THAT AT ONE TO FIFTY!
THAT WAS BEFORE STURMVORAUS EVENED THE ODDS. IT'S ANYONE'S RACE NOW.
REALLY? DEN HY GUN BET FEEFTY ON ME!
...SURE. GOOD LUCK.

MEANWHILE, ON CASTLE WULFENBACH—
OH. HELLO. I THOUGHT I'D BEEN COMPLETELY FORGOTTEN.
SAY—IS THERE ANY WAY I CAN GET A GOLDFISH OR SOMETHING IN HERE?
I'M DEAD BORED.
CHAPTER 10
LEAGUE of The LIVELY DEAD
"KEPT ME UP!"
OG THE IMMORTAL
ZOMG! YOU'RE DEAD! .. NOW WHAT?
WORRY ABOUT THAT.
THERE'S AN EXCELLENT CHANCE SOMEONE WILL TRY TO KILL YOU SOON.
WHAT?! BUT THE BARON SAID HE'D PROTECT ME!
I SAID: "TRY."
NOW, LISTEN. I NEED TO ASK YOU SOMETHING, AND I HAVEN'T GOT MUCH TIME.
THEY THINK I'VE GONE TO GET SOME PAPERS.
OH, SURE. BECAUSE NOW I CAN REALLY CONCENTRATE ON ANYTHING.
TRY. IT'S ABOUT THE WASPS.
THE ONES MADE TO ENSLAVE SPARKS.
OH. YOU...KNOW ABOUT THAT.
OH, YES. BUT EVIDENTLY NOT AS MUCH AS YOU DO.
I...I'VE GLANCED AT SOME NOTES...
MM-HMM. HOW LONG HAVE THEY EXISTED?
I ONLY KNEW OF ONE PROTOTYPE... BUT I UNDERSTOOD IT WAS NEVER RELEASED.
COULD THERE BE MORE?
HMM. THEORETICALLY, YES.
SO HOW LONG?
ER...A YEAR? NO MORE THAN THAT.
HM. LONG ENOUGH...WHY WASN'T IT USED?
THERE WAS A PLAN—
—BUT?
WELL, THE PROJECT WAS OVERSEEN BY SNARLANTZ, IN PASSHOLDT.
PASSHOLDT? AH. I SEE.
YES. A BAD BUSINESS, THAT.
SO, WITH THIS NEW WASP—
COULD AN ENSLAVED SPARK RESIST A DIRECT COMMAND BY THE OTHER?
OF COURSE NOT. THAT'S THE WHOLE POINT.
WHAT IF HE WAS ALREADY IN A FULL-BLOWN SPARK-INDUCED FUGUE STATE?
OH... INTERESTING. I...DON'T KNOW.
BUT IF I HAD TO GUESS—I'D SAY NO.
THAT'S... NOT GOOD ENOUGH.

SOON—
I'M BACK, HERR BARON!
AH. THANK YOU, BORIS.
GENERAL? PLEASE CONTINUE.
CONTINUE?! I HAVEN'T EVEN STARTED!
YOU WANT US TO COMPLETELY REARRANGE OUR STRATEGY! WE'LL HAVE TO REASSIGN ALMOST EVERY UNIT WE HAVE!
THIS NEW PLAN WILL TAKE TIME!
—AND EVERY MILITARY STRATEGIST FOR THE LAST FIVE HUNDRED YEARS WILL TELL YOU: DON'T GIVE THE HETERODYNES TIME!
WHAT'S GOING ON? I WAS ONLY FIVE MINUTES LATE!
WHAT NEW PLAN?
AND HERE WE'RE ALL SET TO JUST LIQUEFY THE PLACE, AND NOW THIS!
"MINIMAL DAMAGE." FEH!
DUE TO THE NEW INFORMATION SOMEBODY BROUGHT IN,
OUR NEW PRIORITY IS TO CAPTURE THE GIRL, ALIVE.
OH, I DOUBT THERE WOULD HAVE BEEN ANYTHING LEFT TO "LIQUEFY" AFTER MY THUNDER BEES HAD CLEARED THE AREA.
OH! WELL, THAT'S...THAT'S GOOD, HERR BARON, BUT...
YOU JUST TOLD YOUR SON THAT THE GIRL HAS TO DIE! WHY—
BORIS. IF YOUR INFORMATION IS CORRECT,
IF SHE IS, HERSELF, INFECTED AS SOME NEW KIND OF "QUEEN" REVENANT—
THEN SHE IS AN INVALUABLE SPECIMEN, AND MUST BE STUDIED.
BUT I DO NOT WANT MY SON TO HARBOR ANY FALSE HOPE.
SHE IS ALREADY AS GOOD AS DEAD.
PLEASE—THOSE THINGS?
YOU WILL COWER BEFORE MY INSECT MIGHT!
FLAMING OIL GUNS RULE!
HOLD STILL! MY MATH SHALL PROVE YOU ALL INADEQUATE!

...AND IN ANOTHER PART OF MECHANICSBURG—
OKAY, PEOPLE! HERE'S THE NEXT ONE!
OI! WHAT THE—PUSH OFF, YOU RABBLE! WE'RE WORKIN' HERE!
Die We
WELL, NOW, SO ARE WE.
WE'RE NOT HERE TO MAKE TROUBLE.
OH, REALLY. WELL, LOOK, YOU—
TROUBLE? I CAN SQUISH...
NO! I TOLD YOU TO STOP THAT!
JEEZ! YOU JUST GOT OUT!
IF YOU BEAT THIS GUY TO DEATH, I'LL GET IN TROUBLE!
SWEET LADY OF SOLDER!
YOU'RE PRISONERS FROM THE CASTLE!
NOT ANY MORE!
NOW WE'RE A ROVING BAND OF HEROIC REPAIRMEN. SEE?!
HEY! THIS IS THE SAME LIST WE'RE WORKING FROM!
AH. I SEE WHY THE CASTLE THOUGHT YOU COULD USE SOME HELP.
DEPARTMENT OF PUBL
PUBLIC WORKS DEPT.
MUST! MPWD
HEY, NOW. WE'VE BEEN UNDER ATTACK, YOU KNOW!
WE'VE HAD MADBOYS BLOWIN' STUFF UP ALL DAY!
DPW
WE'VE BEEN STUCK JUST TRYIN' TO MOVE THIS FOOL STATUE FOR THE LAST TWO HOURS!
SUBSTATION
pft. IF WE LET STUFF LIKE THAT STOP US, WE'D STILL BE INSIDE.
R-79?
YEAH!
WHAM! SMASH! CRRUMBLE
DONE!
DPW
RIGHT. NOW, LET'S GET THIS DONE BEFORE HER ROYAL SPARKINESS SHOWS UP—
AND TURNS US ALL INTO FISH OR SOMETHING.
HER—YOU MEAN THE LADY HETERODYNE?
YOU KNOW HER?

HERR VON ZINZER HERE IS HER CHIEF MINION!
R-REALLY?
UH-HUH.
THE CASTLE SAID SO AND EVERYTHING!
—ONLY UNTIL I CAN CATCH THE FIRST AIRSHIP OUT OF HERE.
NOW, LET'S FIX THIS STUPID THING.
YES SIR! RIGHT AWAY, SIR!
ME AND THE BOYS GOT THIS ONE, SIR!
...THE HECK? NOW WHAT'S GOT INTO THEM?
AH! SIMPLE! YOU OUTRANK THEM!
UH, HOW DO YOU FIGURE?
AS WITH SPARKS, SO WITH MINIONS—
IN ANY GROUP, SOMEONE WILL EMERGE AS "ALPHA."
uh...AL WHO?
HEH. YOU ARE THE LADY HETERODYNE'S CHIEF MINION, THEREFORE ALL OTHER MINIONS ARE SUBORDINATE TO YOU. IT'S FASCINATING, REALLY.
WAIT—YOU'RE SAYING THAT SHE PUSHES ME AROUND, SO I GET TO PUSH EVERYBODY ELSE AROUND?
THAT'S INSANE!
HMM...YOUR POINT?
...DID I SAY AIRSHIP?
NUTS TO THAT. I'LL WALK OUT!
HECK, I'LL RUN!
THERE IS NOTHING THAT'LL KEEP ME—
UM...
EXCUSE ME, BUT...
IS...IS THERE ANYTHING LEFT FOR ME TO DO?

UM—WE'VE GOT AN OIL PUMP WITH A CLOGGED FEED LINE.
I'M ON IT!
SO?
HUH? WHAT?
SO, I THOUGHT SHE WAS YOUR BIG ROMANTICAL IDÉE FIXE.
...UH—IS THERE A BROKEN—?
OH, SHUT UP.
YES, MOST INTERESTING. FOR A LOVE-BESOTTED LOUT, YOU WERE QUITE UNAFFECTED!
DID EVERYONE KNOW ABOUT THAT?!
HM? OH, NOT EVERYONE...
JUST THOSE OF US WHO NOTICED THAT ANYONE WHO GOT TO YOUR KITCHEN AFTER SANAA WAS SERVED BOILED SPONGE WITH GRAVY.
OH. OH, YEAH, I GUESS—
SO? SO? ARE YOU OVER HER NOW? HUH?
I...I DON'T KNOW.
I...EVERYTHING IS SUDDENLY SO DIFFERENT.
I MEAN, I STILL LIKE HER,
OH, REALLY...
BUT SEE—UNTIL THESE LAST FEW DAYS, I NEVER HAD A CHANCE TO GET USED TO BEING AROUND ATTRACTIVE WOMEN!
SO, SANAA? YEAH, SHE'S SMART AND TOUGH AND I LIKE BEING AROUND HER—
BUT SINCE I FEEL THE SAME WAY ABOUT YOU,
I OBVIOUSLY DON'T KNOW ANYTHING ABOUT
STUPID, HUH?
OH, PROFESSOR, I WANT TO KILL SOMETHING SO VERY, VERY MUCH!
MY GOODNESS.
ONE.

HOW'S IT GOING, PROFESSOR?
JUST CLOSING IT UP, MY BOY!
DID YOU SAY THIS WAS THE *LAST ONE?*
THAT'S WHAT I *SAID,* YES...
<sigh.> BUT I DIDN'T *BELIEVE* IT.
AH! *THERE* YOU ARE, HERR VON ZINZER! *WELL DONE!*
BRING YOUR TEAM TO THE GUARD HOUSE JUST INSIDE THE CATHEDRAL GATE. I HAVE FOUND MORE WORK FOR YOU!
GAH! IT'S THE *CASTLE!*
AH. NO DOUBT YOU FORESAW THAT EACH REPAIR WOULD ALLOW IT TO SEE THE *NEXT* PROBLEM, YES?
NO, I JUST KNOW THAT IT *HATES ME!*
WE'LL BE DOING THIS *FOREVER!*
HMF. LOOKS LIKE *YOU'VE* BEEN A *BUSY* LITTLE LAB RAT.
PARDON ME? *I* WAS JUST GETTING AN *ASSIGNMENT.*
OH *REALLY?* WELL, I HAVEN'T NOTICED *YOU* WASTING ANY TIME.
GET THE ONE YOU *WANT?*
OH, TOO BAD. I GUESS *NOT,* HUH?
I HEAR NOTHING...
I SEE NOTHING...
WELL, THERE... THERE *HAS* TO BE AN END AT *SOME POINT...*
SORRY? WHAT PART OF THE TOWN FULL OF RUBBLE ARE *YOU* LOOKING AT?
SHH—*WAIT.* QUIET...
EVERYONE! ***HIT THE GROUND!***

UH—
WHAT THE—IT'S C-GAS!
PONK!
HMF. STUPID. A LITTLE THING LIKE THIS?
JUST COVER IT UP, YES?
THUNK!
OOOH.
UH-OH.
PONK!
PONK!
PONK!

AUGH! NOT AGAIN—
GAS? DON'T WORRY, THE BOYS IN CENTRAL WILL GET IT!
JUST HOLD YOUR BREATH FOR A MINUTE.
HOLD MY—WHEN WAS THAT EVER GOOD AGAINST C-GAS?!
TRUST ME!
FFFWOOSH!
SPLOOSH!
FSSSSH!
PONK!
PONK!
PONK!
PONK!
PONK!
PONK!
PONK!
PONK!
PONK!
WHAT THE—WHAT WAS THAT?!
AETHERIC PARTICLE NEUTRALIZING HYDRO-ATMOSPHERIC DRENCH!
WE GOT IT FIXED AND PRIMED THIS MORNING!
WAIT...LIKE IN A LAB? IT...IT COVERS THE WHOLE TOWN?
SURE! A TOWN RUN BY THE HETERODYNES, ATTACKED ON A REGULAR BASIS FOR HUNDREDS OF YEARS?
GAS WEAPONS ARE EASY!
IF WE HAVE TO, WE CAN LAUNCH ENTIRE BUILDINGS AT ATTACKERS!
AND YOU PEOPLE PUT UP WITH THIS?
JEEZ, IT'S NOT LIKE IT HAPPENS EVERY DAY.

RIGHT. GET MOVING BEFORE THEY DROP ANYTHING *ELSE* ON US.
WITH ALL THOSE STORM CLOUDS, *ANYTHING* COULD BE UP THERE.
EH, IT CAN'T BE *THAT BAD.*
OH?
SURE. IF THERE WERE A *REAL* THREAT, THE *TORCHMEN*—
THOSE THINGS? THEY'RE CONTROLLED BY THE *CASTLE,* AREN'T THEY?
THE CASTLE THAT'S BEEN WHINGING THAT IT'S GOT NO POWER TO DO ANYTHING *USEFUL* RIGHT NOW?
UH—
SO, THIS NEXT LOCATION—
IT GOT A *BASEMENT?*
...A NICE *DEEP* ONE.
LET'S GO.

AERIAL BOMBARDMENT FROM HIGH ALTITUDE.
MUST BE AIRSHIPS UP THERE—
OR...OR *SOMETHING*.
BOOM! BOOM!
THAT'LL BE WHAT THE TORCHMEN ARE AFTER.
AND ALL THOSE LIGHTS— THAT'LL BE THE TORCHMEN TAKING 'EM OUT.
...I *HOPE*.
SHOULD WE STILL BE UP HERE? IT SEEMS A BIT *DANGEROUS*.
IT'LL BE WORSE DOWN THERE, LAD.
BESIDES, *SOMEBODY'S* GOT TO KEEP WATCH. THIS WAY, WE CAN WARN PEOPLE IF SOMETHING *HAPPENS*.
*!

AAAH!
GIANT MONKEY!
YES, YES, CALM DOWN.
UH—
COWER ON YOUR OWN TIME, LACKEY!
I AM CORNELIUS SENEAR—
MASTER OF ANTHROPOID AVIATION!
I SEEK ASYLUM FOR MYSELF AND MY BEAUTIFUL AEROAPES!
ASYLUM. REALLY.
YES, YES! I ADMIT IT!
WHEN I HEARD OLD KLAUS WAS WEAKENED, I ATTEMPTED TO PRESS MY ADVANTAGE!
I CANNOT BE BLAMED FOR THIS!
THERE WAS A POWER VACUUM!
I HAD AN UNSTOPPABLE ARMY OF AEROAPES!
LOGIC AND SCIENCE DEMANDED THAT I WREST CONTROL OF THE EMPIRE!
BUT ALAS, IT APPEARS I MADE MY MOVE TOO SOON.
THE BARON HAS RETURNED, AND HAS BLOWN MY UNSTOPPABLE ARMY FROM THE SKIES!
THE BARON IS ALIVE?!
OH, YES. AND HE'S ANGRY! HE DIDN'T EVEN TRY TO CAPTURE US ALIVE!
MAYBE HE'S JUST OUT OF PATIENCE.
WHAT- BECAUSE OF ME?!
BECAUSE OF ALL OF YOU.
HOY! YOU!
DOCTOR IGNEOUS SLAGHAMMER AND HIS BEAUTIFUL CLAW SEEK ASYLUM!
REJOICE!

BY SIR ISAAC! THE TORCHMEN!
I NEVER THOUGHT I'D SEE THEM!
BUT—THAT MEANS—
IT MEANS THERE'S SOMETHING UP THERE. ABOVE THE CLOUDS.
RIGHT. IT LOOKS LIKE WE GOT TO THIS THING JUST IN TIME.
LET'S HOPE WE CAN KEEP THE POWER FLOWING LONG ENOUGH TO GET RID OF IT—WHATEVER IT IS.
WELL...WE SHOULD BE ABLE TO—
MAYBE—
ASSUMING NOTHING ELSE ATTACKS WHILE THE TORCHMEN ARE UP.
VERY TRUE, MY LADY, BUT YOU ARE DOING WELL.
CASTLE! SHOULD YOU BE TALKING?
NOT REALLY... BUT YOUR MINIONS HAVE JUST RECONNECTED THE COAL GAS LINES-
AND I NOW REMEMBER MANY OTHER THINGS THAT WILL BE VERY USEFUL!
SOON, WE MAY ACTUALLY HAVE A CHANCE.
HO. AZ LONG AS HYU DUN FIRE OP DOSE ELECTRIC VEEL TINGS.
HM? "ELECTRIC WHEEL THINGS?" NOW THAT SOUNDS INTRIGUING!
TELL ME MORE!
NEFFER HEARD OV DEM!
NO SOCH TING!
HY VOS JUST KIDDING!
OOOH. VERY INTRIGUING!
SO, AT THIS POINT, WITH EVERYTHING WE'VE DONE SO FAR, AND THE COAL GAS LINES YOU MENTIONED,
WHAT ARE YOU CAPABLE OF?
MM. RIGHT NOW, JUST THIS.
I AM RESERVING JUST ENOUGH POWER TO MAINTAIN MY HIGHER CONSCIOUSNESS,
BUT THAT WILL BE SACRIFICED IN AN EMERGENCY.
RRRUMBLE!
WHAAA! THE GROUND IS SHAKING!
CASTLE! WHAT'S HAPPENING?!
OH, DEAR...
CASTLE?
PLEASE ENJOY THIS MUSICAL INTERLUDE... TYMPANUS HETERODYNE'S SYMPHONY #7: MORE BIG DRUMS AND SCREAMING.

MEANWHILE—
UGH. YOU DIDN'T SAY WE WERE GOING INSIDE THE CATHEDRAL.
THIS PLACE CREEPS ME OUT.
WITH A NAME LIKE "MOLOCH?"
I'M NOT SURPRISED.
I'M HELPING!
'S WRONG WITH MY NAME?
MY MOTHER PICKED IT OUT OF THE WHACHAMACALIT—THE BIBLE.
AH.
UM—DID SHE READ IT?
CAN I SOLDER THESE TOGETHER?
YES I CAN!
NAH. I HAD EIGHT BROTHERS. NOBODY HAD TIME FOR STUFF LIKE THAT ON THE FARM.
OH, YEAH. THAT'S PRETTY COMMON.
I'M HELPING!
...BUT WHY DON'T YOU LIKE OUR CATHEDRAL?
...HAVE YOU KIDS EVER BEEN OUT OF MECHANICSBURG?
CHAPEL of JOY
YOU'RE ONE OF THOSE MILITANT AGNOSTICS THE ABBESS WARNS US ABOUT, AREN'T YOU?
HELPING!
CALL THIS A WAR? I DO NOT. WHERE ARE THE MONSTERS?
PFT. HAVE YOU SEEN THE MINIONS THEY GET TODAY? YOU JUST CANNOT GET THE RIGHT PARTS.
CATHEDRAL FUND GIVE

RRRUMBLE!
AK! WHAT—
RUN, CHILDREN! FLEE! FLEE!
IT'S NOT STOPPING!
DID— DID WE DO THIS?!
NO! WELL...I SUPPOSE WE COULD HAVE, BUT...
SHUT UP AND GET TO THE COURTYARD!
NOW!
VREEEOW!
OOPS.
WHAT DID YOU DO TO MY CATHEDRAL?
THAT WASN'T US!

WELL, BLESS MY BOILERS!
THAT'S ONE OF YOUNG ISKENSHOD'S SUBMERSIBLES DE TERRE!
FWHUMP!
HE WAS A STUDENT OF MINE, YOU KNOW.
IT'S STRANGE TO SEE ONE ABOVE THE GROUND LIKE THIS—
THEY REALLY AREN'T DESIGNED FOR—
K-RUUNCH!
RUNCH
RUNCH
RUNCH!
OHHHH! *FLEEING FROM AN ENEMY!*
OF COURSE! IT ALL MAKES SENSE, NOW!
OH, OF *COURSE*.
UH, MA'AM? FOR WHAT IT'S WORTH, WE DON'T KNOW ANYTHING ABOUT *THAT*, EITHER.
tsk. OF *COURSE NOT*.
OUR CATACOMBS ARE CONNECTED TO THE OLD KRAKEN WORKS CAVERNS.
—ALWAYS *KNEW* THERE WERE STILL A FEW OF THOSE DEVILS DOWN THERE.
SO, UM, IF WE PROMISE NOT TO CAUSE ANY MORE MECHANICAL WHALE ATTACKS—
CAN WE GO INSIDE AND GET BACK TO WORK?
WELL

VREEEOW!
VREEEOW!
RUNCH
VREEEOW
NO, REALLY, SERIOUSLY. *WE* DID *NOT* CAUSE THAT.
WOW! HOW MANY OF THEM *ARE* THERE?
AMAZING! THEY'RE ABLE TO MANEUVER ON THE *SURFACE!*
THESE ARE NO *ORDINARY* SUBTERRANEAN MECHA-NARWHALS!
...RIGHT.
THIS IS ONLY GOING TO GET *WORSE*.
GET YOUR PEOPLE BACK TO WORK—AND WORK *FAST*.
KEEPER SVEK— I WANT THE CHILDREN REMOVED TO THE VAULTS BENEATH THE IRON CRYPTS.
YES, ABBESS.
THEN HAVE THE GROOMS BRING OUT MY CHARGER, AND—*OH*—
BE SURE TO SHOW THESE PEOPLE THE *BLOODSTONE PALADINS*.
IF THEY CAN GET THEM *WORKING*, I WANT THEM EQUIPPED FOR *SUSTAINED SMITING!*

MEANWHILE—
WHAT IS HE DOING?!
WHO?
THE BARON, OBVIOUSLY.
UM... ATTACKING US?
WELL, HE'S DOING A TERRIBLE JOB OF IT!
HOW SO?
HALF THE EMPIRE'S SPECIAL UNITS ARE BEATING AT OUR GATES!
I'VE JUST HAD A REPORT THAT A SUBTERRANEAN FORCE HAS SURFACED NEAR THE CATHEDRAL!
THE CASTLE CAN ONLY DEFEND ONE FRONT AT A TIME—
AND IT CAN'T EVEN DO THAT FOREVER!
AT THIS POINT, THERE SHOULDN'T BE GATES!
OR A CATHEDRAL! OR A CASTLE!
HE WAS ALL SET TO VAPORIZE THIS PLACE!
THE ONLY THING STOPPING HIM WAS HIS SON'S PRESENCE HERE—
AND ACCORDING TO STURMVORAUS, HE'S BACK ON CASTLE WULFENBACH—PROBABLY UNDER LOCK AND KEY.
SO WHAT IS THE BARON UP TO?
IF HYU DUN DESTROY A TARGET, IZ BECAUZE DERE IZ SUMTING HYU VANT STILL IN IT.
YES—BUT WHAT?
MAYBE HE VANT DE LADY HETERODYNE ALIVE AFTER ALL.
...IT MIGHT NOT BE ME—
IT COULD BE THE CASTLE!
OR THE LIBRARY!
OR...OR THE JÄGERS! OR—
OCCAM'S RAZOR!
YES, YOU'RE RIGHT, OF COURSE—
HIT VOS FORGED BY OLD OCCAM HETERODYNE!
AH... WHAT?
SERIOUSLY—WHO VOULDN'T VANT IT?
HOO—DOT TING KEN CU THROUGH ANYTING!

SOON—
...THE BARON'S GOT MORE EFFECTIVE FORCES JUST SITTING OUT THERE *WAITING*.
WHY?!
THAT'S WHAT WE'RE GOING TO FIND OUT.
WE'LL START BY TAKING A LOOK AT THE MACHINES ATTACKING THE CATHEDRAL.
IT'S JUST...THE EMPIRE STAYS TOGETHER BECAUSE PEOPLE *KNOW* KLAUS IS TOO POWERFUL TO CHALLENGE.
HE'S PUTTING THAT PERCEPTION INTO QUESTION.
WELL, EVERYONE KNOWS THE BARON DOESN'T *CARE* WHAT PEOPLE THINK OF HIM.
HE *NEVER HAS*.
THAT'S BECAUSE HE'S ALWAYS BEEN STRONG ENOUGH TO DO AS HE LIKES!
BUT NOW— ACCORDING TO STURMVORAUS, THERE ARE UPRISINGS ALL OVER THE EMPIRE.
THERE IS A REAL POSSIBILITY OF ACTUAL DAMAGE TO HIS RULE—
AND THE BARON IS *LETTING IT HAPPEN*.
NO— SOMETHING IS GOING ON HERE!
ALL RIGHT. I GET IT. FOR SOME REASON, HE'S SENDING WEAK STUFF AGAINST US.
HE'S NOT WEAK, AND HE'S NOT STUPID, SO OBVIOUSLY, HE'S *UP TO SOMETHING*.
FINE. UNTIL WE FIGURE OUT *WHAT*, WE GET MORE TIME... AND I GET MORE *PRACTICE*.
WATCH THIS!
CRASH!
HEY!

REJOICE! THE HETERODYNE HAS RETURNED!
THRUNCH!
UM... THANK YOU?
EH. JUST DOIN' MY JOB.
SAY, AREN'T YOU THE HETERODYNE?
...YES?
THOUGHT SO. RECOGNIZED THE ARMOR.
PLEASURE TO MEET'CHA.
YOU'LL WANT TO ROLL AROUND IN THE TREASURE, I EXPECT?
SMEK!
WELL... AFTER THE INVASION PERHAPS?
TCH. OH, NO, THAT'S FINE-TAKE YOUR TIME, MISTRESS...
I'LL JUST GO DO SOME MORE FIGHTING, I GUESS.
HEY, YOU!
REJOICE!

KRAKLE!
BOOM!
WHOA. THAT DOESN'T SOUND GOOD.
NO, IT DOESN'T. CASTLE?
I REQUIRE... A... SPARK...
AH... WHAT?
I REQUIRE... A... SPARK...
CASTLE-I AM A SPARK. WHAT DO YOU NEED?
I REQUIRE... A... SPARK...
WHAT SHOULD I DO?
I REQUIRE... A... SPARK...
I'VE NEVER HEARD IT LIKE THIS. WHAT'S WRONG?
OH, NO.
IT'S... BECOME TOO WEAK...
BUT...A SPARK?
DOES IT MEAN AGATHA?
I MEAN, FOR THE CASTLE, THE HETERODYNE'S THE ONLY SPARK THAT MATTERS...
I REQUIRE... A... SPARK...
AND SHE'S ALREADY DONE SO MUCH. WHAT ELSE CAN SHE DO?
I DON'T KNOW.
WE'VE MANAGED TO KEEP THE CASTLE GOING LONGER THAN WE THOUGHT POSSIBLE, AND NOW THE ATTACKS ARE COMING FROM TOO MANY SIDES.
THE CASTLE HAS BEEN TRYING TO DO TOO MUCH-BURNING ENERGY TOO FAST.
OUR BEST DEFENSES ARE ABOUT TO SHUT DOWN COMPLETELY.

I TOLD YOU, I HAVE A PLAN.
USING HYUSELF AS BAIT IZ NOT A GOOT PLAN!
HYU GOTS AN ARMY NOW.
HYU VANT TO KNOW VOT'S GOINK ON VIT DE BARON?
DEN HYU GETS US TO PONCH SOMEBODY UNTIL DEY TELLS US.
JUST MAKE IZ SOMBODDY VIT SCHMOTTS.
DEM SCHTUPID VIND-OP VALE TINGS VON'T TELL HYU NOTTING!
FLEE, COWARDLY PEASANTS!
I, DOCTOR GALLIARD PRUNESTOGGLE, MASTER OF-
ER-MASTER OF... NOTHING IMPORTANT, REALLY.
FINE. HE TALKS A LOT.
PUNCH HIM.
WAIT-SURELY WE CAN DISCUSS THIS.
ALL RIGHT, WHAT'S THE BARON UP TO?
WHAT? I DON'T KNOW!
AIEEE!
THIS IS... UNSATISFYING.
LIKE BEING DE LEADER, SVEETIE.

VOOHOO!
WHOO! HY MISSED DIS!
VOT, DIS BEEG GUY?
HE VOS FUN, BUT HY DUN TINK VE'S SEEN HIM BEFORE—
NAW, HY MEAN FIGHTIN' VIT DE PACK AGAIN!
HO. DOT. YAH, DOT'S NIZE.
YAH! HY JUST HOPE DE ODDERS DUN GET TOO JEALOUS—VOT VIT HAVING LEGENDARY HERO-TYPE GUYZ LIKE US AROUND ALL DE TIME, HEY?
VE...VE IZ VOT NOW?
VELL, HY GOT'S OL' MAN DEATH'S HAT!
DOT MAKES ME SOME PREDDY HOT SCHTUFF, HYU KNOW!
UND ALL DOT AWESOMENESS GOTS TO RUB OFF ON HYU GUYZ AT LEAST A LIDDLE BIT, YAH?
HEY DERE, BRODDERS! VE'S MAKIN' A LIST!
IF HYU VANTS TO FIGHT MAXIM FOR HIZ HAT—
HY KIN PUT HYU DOWN FOR NOMBERS TREE-NINEY-SIX AN' TREE-NINEY-SEFFEN!
SIGN ME OP.
HEH. HY TINK VE'S GUN GET MORE DEN AWESOMENESS RUBBED OFF ON US.

THE BARON'S LARGER PLAN?
WE... WE DO NOT KNOW THE LARGER PLAN!
WHAT ARE YOU IMPLYING?
WE ARE A SPECIAL GROUP! HAND-PICKED BY THE BARON HIMSELF!
HE SAID TO ME: "ONLY YOUR UNIQUE TALENTS ARE UP TO THIS IMPORTANT AND MOST DELICATE OF TASKS!"
-SEIZE THE HETERODYNE GIRL-
-SEIZE THE HETERODYNE GIRL-
-SEIZE THE HETERODYNE GIRL-
A.5.0
tch. HOW MANY PEOPLE WITH "UNIQUE TALENTS" DOES THE BARON HAVE?
THEY'RE ALL SAYING THE SAME THING.
HMM...HY IZ GUESSING... LOTS.
FOR SUM REASON, KLAUS IZ TURNINK LOOSE ALL HIZ DUCKIEST QVAKS.
STILL, THERE ARE SO MANY OF THEM...
NOT TO MENTION THE ARMY AT THE GATES...
VUN TING AT A TIME, MISTRESS. ENNYVAY, HAFF OV DESE GUYS VILL FALL APART VUNCE DE RAIN SCHTARTS.
SERIOUSLY?
HYU'VE SEEN DEEZ GUYS. VE'S DOINK DEM A KINDNESS,
KNOCKIN' DEM DOWN IN A GOOT FIGHT.
WELL, I CAN BE KIND...
AGATHA!

I REQUIRE... A... SPARK...
...AND IT'S JUST BEEN *REPEATING THIS?*
I REQUIRE... A... SPARK...
YES! IT'S COMPLETELY UNRESPONSIVE.
I'D HOPED THAT IF WE BROUGHT *YOU* HERE—
CITY PUMP
Nº 6
FACTORY
HM...A "SPARK OF LIFE" MAYBE?
YOU *SAID* WE'RE NEARLY OUT OF *POWER.*
WE *ARE.* THE CASTLE'S BEEN KEEPING OFF THE MAIN ATTACKS—
BUT OBVIOUSLY, THINGS ARE *ALREADY* SLIPPING THROUGH.
IF THE BARON GIVES ONE MORE BIG PUSH, THAT'LL BE *IT.*
WE'VE ALREADY SHUNTED EVERY POWER SOURCE WE CAN *THINK OF* OVER TO THE CASTLE.
IT JUST ISN'T *ENOUGH.*
I REQUIRE... A... SPARK...
YES, *YES!* I *KNOW! AND YOU'VE GOT LOTS OF THEM!*
... BUT AT *THIS POINT,* THE ONLY USEFUL THING TO DO THAT *I* CAN THINK OF IS *GRIND THEM UP AND BURN THEM FOR FUEL!*
I REQUIRE... A... SPARK...
OH. NO, SORRY, I WAS ONLY—
I MEAN, I ONLY MEANT—
MY GOODNESS, YOUNG MAN! I AM *IMPRESSED!*
ASSUMING WE ALL SURVIVE, YOU *MUST* COME WORK WITH *US!*
OH, YES! YOU HAVE THE MAKINGS OF ONE OF THE *GREATS!*

WAIT—DO YOU HEAR THAT? WHAT *NOW?*
THANK YOU FOR COWERIN SHOPPING!
BOOOM!
MY LADY! THE BARON'S FORCES HAVE BROUGHT IN A *BATTERING RAM!*
WILL THE GATES *HOLD?*
I HOPE SO, BECAUSE THIS IS IT. THE CASTLE IS *DONE.*
BOOOM!
AGATHA...
I KNOW. BUT THEY HAVEN'T GOT THROUGH YET.
WE HAVE EVERYONE IN TOWN AS ORGANIZED AND READY AS WE'RE GOING TO GET THEM,
SO COME ON—
WE'RE GOING UP TO THE TOP OF THE WALLS.
I WANT TO SEE WHAT'S HAPPENING,
AND MAYBE WE CAN FIND SOMETHING UP THERE TO *DROP ON THEIR HEADS.*

IT'S A RAM.
HY KNOWS VOT IT IZ! HY VANTS TO KNOW HOW IT GOTS SO CLOSE!
HOW SHOULD I KNOW?
WITH ALL THE SMOKE AND CHAOS OUT THERE, IT'S A MIRACLE WE HAVE ANY INTELLIGENCE AT ALL.
GDUN GDUN GDUN GDUN GDUN GDUN GDUN
GENERAL! HOW BAD IS IT?
AH! LADY HETERODYNE!
IT'S A RAM.
SO I'VE BEEN TOLD. IS THERE ANYTHING WE CAN DO?
BRACE HYUSELF!
WHAT—
AAH! IT'S A RAM!
HO YEZ. AT LEAST IT AIN'T VUN OV DE VUNS VOT BREATHE FIRE.
DOSE VUNS VOS ALVAYS HEXPLODEINK VEN DEY HIT.

BOOOM!
WHAT HAVE WE GOT THAT CAN STOP IT?
DOT'S TRICKY.
ALL OUR REALLY GOOT SCHTUFF DUN VORK.
UND VOT DOES VORK IZ EITHER TOO SCHMALL TO DEAL VIT ALL DOT,
OR BEEG ENUFF TO BLOW OUR OWN VALLS DOWN AT DIS RANGE.

I DO NOT LIKE THIS.
VAT? MY HEND?
NO, NO—JUST LOOK AT THIS ARMY.
IZ PRETTY MEZZED OP, ALL RIGHT. VE GOTS TO BE DOIN' SOMETING RIGHT.
US? PLEASE. WE HAVEN'T DONE ENOUGH TO CAUSE THIS! IT'S SHEER CHAOS!
BOT...DOT IZ GOOT FOR UZ, YEZ?
IT DOESN'T MAKE SENSE! THE BARON'S DEPLOYMENTS ARE ALWAYS ORDERED AND EFFICIENT!
HO! BUT DEY'S SAYINK DE BARON IS MISSINK! MAYBE DEAD!
STILL—
HY SEE DIS SORT OV TING BEFORE. AFTER DE BIG BOSS GETS SQVASHED, EFFRY LEEDLE BOSS START TO TINK HE GOTS TO BE DE VUN TO TAKE CHARGE!
UND DEY ALL ACTS LIKE LEETLE KEEDS IN AN...IN AN...OH VOT'S DOT VORD...?
...KINDERGARTEN?
ABATTOIR!
...NOW YOU MOVE YOUR HAND.
HO...WRONG VORD, HUH?

BOOM!
RIGHT. WE'RE OUT OF TIME. I'LL JUST GET IN MY ARMOR, OPEN THE GATES, AND ***FRY*** IT ***HEAD-ON.***
HUH. EKTUALLY, HIT LOOK LIKE HYU VON'T HAFF TO DO ***DOT***...
AGATHA!
BEHOLD, O DARK MISTRESS! YOUR RIDICULOUSLY FEARSOME BATTLE ARMOR AWAITS!
TARVEK! HOW ON EARTH DID YOU GET ***THAT*** UP HERE?!
HASTILY-IMPROVISED ROCKET BOOSTERS!
QUICK SAFETY TIP: DON'T CLICK YOUR HEELS UNLESS YOU
SO, WOULD MY LADY LIKE TO TAKE OVER?
I'VE RECHARGED GIL'S LIGHTNING STICK. YOU CAN BLOW THAT MONSTER TO ***GYROS*** WITH THIS THING!
THAT'S ALL RIGHT, YOU GO AHEAD.
WHAT, REALLY? BUT IT'S YOUR TOWN...
TRUE. BUT YOU LOOK LIKE YOU'RE HAVING FUN. I'LL GET THE ***NEXT ONE.***
YOU KNOW, IF WE ***LIVE,*** I CAN DESIGN YOU SOMETHING ***BETTER*** THAN THIS—
BETTER? IT'S A TWO-TON MOBILE ARMORED ***DEATH KNIGHT SUIT.***
WHAT COULD MAKE IT ***BETTER?***
...NICER CURVES? IN ***GREEN?***
RAM. THEN WE'LL TALK.

ZZKRAK!
SKRAZZZK!
IT...IT'S STILL COMING!
AGATHA! LOOK OUT!
BOOOM!
KRASH!
WHAT THE DEVIL?! THAT WAS A DIRECT HIT!
THEY'VE... THEY'VE SHIELDED IT!
I WAS AFRAID OF THIS.
EVERYONE SAW GIL USE THE STICK—
IT MAKES SENSE THAT THE BARON WOULD HAVE WORKED OUT SOME KIND OF DEFENSE AGAINST IT.

SO NOW, THE *CASTLE'S* USELESS, AND THE *LIGHTNING STICK* IS USELESS—
NOT NECESSARILY. ONCE WE GET THOSE GENERATOR TOWERS GIL SET UP ON THE WALLS RUNNING—
NO—RIGHT NOW, AT THIS VERY MOMENT, THEY COUNT AS *USELESS.*
OY! SOMETHING'S *HAPPENING!*
THEY'RE PULLING BACK THE *RAM!*
WHAT? BUT THAT'S...OH. THAT'S *NOT GOOD.*
IT'S NOT?
BUT THE GATES HELD—
IT MEANS THAT, QUITE PROBABLY, ALL THIS WAS A *TEST.*
THE BARON HAS BEEN SENDING ALL THESE THINGS AGAINST US—
EACH SLIGHTLY STRONGER THAN THE LAST.
WATCHING TO SEE WHAT WE DO.
NOW, HE KNOWS WHAT WE CAN'T STOP.
SO, HYU TINK HE GUN SEND IN AN ARMY OV *BEEG SHEEPS?*
NO—
MECHANICSBURG! HEED MY WORDS!
OH.
WELL.
I THINK IT'LL BE SOMETHING
DIFFERENT.

IF YOU WOULD HAVE ME SPARE YOUR MISERABLE TOWN-
YOU WILL SEND FORTH THE HETERODYNE GIRL-NOW!
OR YOU MAY ATTEMPT TO HIDE HER, IF YOU WISH-AND I WILL RAZE YOUR FILTHY HOVELS TO THE GROUND!
MAKE YOUR CHOICE QUICKLY!
FOR MY PART, I CONTEMPLATE THE DESTRUCTION OF THIS VILE DEN OF PERFIDY WITH GREAT JOY!
HUH. DOT'S NOT GOOT— DOSE GUYS VOS ALVAYS A REAL PAIN IN DE BECKSIDE.
HY THOT VE TOOK CARE OV ALL OV DEM A COUPLE HUNNRED YEARS AGO.
IT'S STUPID. IT'S NOT LIKE SHE'S JUST GOING TO WALK OUT THERE AFTER ALL THIS.
WELL, I HOPE IT WON'T COME TO THAT, BUT...
IF I CAN'T FIGURE OUT WHAT TO DO ABOUT THE CASTLE...
WHO-WHAT THE-WHAT IS THIS?!
OH, NO YOU DON'T, PRETTY BOY!

MY TOWN!
MINE!
AH! BUT WHAT IS THIS?
OBSERVE, MY DEAR GAZPACHO--'TIS A POOR, BASE-BORN LIZARD WITH DREAMS OF DRAGONHOOD!
IN TRUTH, M'LORD, HE IS LARGER THAN ANY LIZARD I HAVE EVER SEEN...
PAH! IF SUPERFICIAL RESEMBLANCES ARE ALL IT TAKES, THEN YOU SIT ASTRIDE HIS DAM!
HAW! GOOD ONE, M'LORD!
OH... OH, YEAH? WELL, WE GOTS MORE THAN ENOUGH REAL DRAGON HERE FOR ONE TOWN, SO YOU AND YOUR LONG-EARED AUNTIE THERE CAN JUST PUSH OFF!
NOW!
TSK. ARE YOU FINISHED, PEASANT?
CLEARLY, YOU ARE NAUGHT BUT A SIDESHOW WONDER- SPRUNG FROM THE FEVERED BLASPHEMIES OF SOME HALF-WIT STUDENT OF OUTDATED ALCHEMY!
UH-
WOT? BUT-I MEAN, AREN'T WE ALL?
FIRE IS NOT HOW TRUE DRAGONS DUEL.
OH, GREAT. LET ME GUESS. THIS IS WHERE YOU SPOUT A BUNCH OF FANCY RIDDLES AND STUFF.
NO.
THIS IS WHERE I PRETTY MUCH JUST BEAT YOU TO DEATH.

GUH...
...
VERILY, M'LORD,
IT HATH TAKEN BUT ONE HIT TO MAKE YOUR POINT.
NO.
ARE YOU NOT FRANZ SCORTCHMAW-BONE GNAWER OF THE HETERODYNES?!
FIRST AND MOST DREAD OF DRAGONS?
YOU BETTER BELIEVE IT, YOU-
...AND YET YOU SWALLOW PETTY INSULTS AND MOVE LIKE A DRUNKEN BOVINE?!
FIGHT ME! FIGHT ME!
I CAME FOR A BATTLE BETWEEN DRAGONS! NOT THIS MUMMER'S PLAY!
YOU WANNA FIGHT?
THEN-
WHAM

SIGH. SO EASY.
YOU ARE NAUGHT BUT A SAMDED SPIT-FROG AFTER ALL, YES?
BOOM!
YOU FANCY-PANTS SHINY-ARSED TWERP-
YER ALL SPARKLE AND TALK.
RUUNCH
LOTS AND LOTS AND LOTS OF TALK!
URK!
CRAK
SO SLOW! IT'S AS IF YOU WERE A SPINELESS SOMNAMBULIST WHO HAS BUT SLEPT FOR YEARS UPON LONG YEARS!
OH... WAIT...
OW... BUT... S' WOT I'M S'POSE T' DO!
...WAITIN' FOR TH' HETERODYNE!
HO! THEN YOU MAY SLEEP AGAIN, AND AWAIT HER BUT A VERY SHORT WHILE LONGER-
IN THE UNDISCOVERED COUNTRY!

AH—HE'S DOWN...
STAND BACK!
AGATHA?
HA! I'M GOING TO TEST SOMETHING!
...WELL—IT'S WORTH A TRY, I GUESS,
BUT ANYTHING THE BARON SENDS IN IS PROBABLY JUST AS SHIELDED AS THAT RAM—
IT'S NOT FOR THEM.
AH-HERR FRANZ-
IF THIS DOESN'T WORK, WELL, THEN... AH... SORRY...
KRZZZK
GRAK!
OH? AND WHAT IS THIS?!
GADZOOKS! IT SEEMS EVEN YOUR OWN TOWN DOESN'T LIKE YOU VERY MUCH!
VERILY, M'LORD, HE HAS BEEN FRIED!
OH, NO-
I FEEL GREAT!

WHAK!
IN FACT,
I HAVEN'T FELT THIS GOOD IN YEARS!
GAHH!
I NEED MORE POWER. YOU! TELL VAN I NEED GIL'S GENERATORS TURNED ON! ALL OF THEM!
I ONLY NEED ONE QUICK BURST, BUT I NEED IT BIG.
AH! YES, LADY!
AGATHA? WHAT ARE YOU PLANNING?
LISTEN–ALL THE HETERODYNE CREATIONS I'VE SEEN–THEY ALL SEEM TO NEED RECHARGING.
THE TORCHMEN, THE MOBILE FUN UNITS, FRANZ, EVEN ADAM AND LILITH NEEDED A JOLT NOW AND THEN.
OOF!
WHUMP
I'LL BET IT'S THE SAME FOR THE CASTLE.
YOU–YOU ARE SOME KIND OF UNHOLY MONSTER!
BY ALL RIGHTS, YOU SHOULD BE DEAD!
THAT'S RIGHT, PAL. I'M A HETERODYNE MONSTER!
–AND THAT'S ONE REEALLY FANCY HAT YOU'VE GOT THERE!
I CAN'T WAIT TO SEE HOW IT LOOKS ON–
POF! POF! POF!
HOLD!
WHOA.
WOT THE–

CEASE THIS OBSTREPEROUS BRAWLING.
YOUR ANTICS SHAME THE LADY HETERODYNE.
AH-SOME OF YOUR... FRIENDS?
DON'T BE INSULTING.
THEY'RE KNIGHTS!

WE ARE HERE TO *RESCUE* THE LADY HETERODYNE AND HER LANDS—
IN THE NAME OF THE *STORM KING!*
THAT VOICE—
THOSE ARE *YOUR* KNIGHTS?
NO!
WELL, I GUESS, *SORT OF...*
THEY *ARE* THE *KNIGHTS OF JOVE.*
...BUT I THOUGHT YOU SAID GIL TOOK THEM ALL OUT WITH THAT *STICK* OF HIS!
THEY *SAID* THEY WERE KNIGHTS OF JOVE, BUT *THAT* WAS AN ARMY OF BIG WAR STOMPERS.
THERE WAS NOTHING LIKE *THESE GUYS.*
VELL, DESE VUNS GOTS GOOT TIMING, ENNYVAY.
OH.
OH.
OF COURSE.
TARVEK?
THE BARON.
THAT PERFECT MESS OF A BATTLEFIELD.
HE'S...HE'S JUST BEEN *WAITING* UNTIL—
FINALLY. THE *TRUE PLAYERS* HAVE *SHOWN THEMSELVES.*

CASTLE WULFENBACH—
I AM IMPRESSED.
YOU SPOTTED THE CONNECTION BEFORE ANYONE ELSE.
EVEN MYSELF.
BECAUSE YOU FIGURED OUT THEIR PURPOSE WHEN YOU DID, I NOW HAVE ALL THE EMPIRE'S GREATEST PROBLEMS IN ONE PLACE, AND SURROUNDED.
WELL DONE.
NOW—
I AM TOLD YOU HAVE ALREADY MADE THREE VERY NEARLY SUCCESSFUL ATTEMPTS TO ESCAPE,
HAVE INJURED SEVERAL GUARDS,
AND RESISTED ALL ATTEMPTS TO BEGIN ANY KIND OF PRELIMINARY TREATMENT.
THIS WILL NOT DO.
BECAUSE OF HER HOLD ON YOU, YOU SHOULD BE INCAPABLE OF DOING ANYTHING TO HARM THE GIRL, SO LISTEN WELL.
I AM ABOUT TO LEVEL MECHANICSBURG, AND DESTROY ITS ALLIES.
THE HETERODYNE GIRL WILL DIE, AS SHE SHOULD.
...BUT YOU CAN SAVE HER.
COOPERATE WITH OUR ATTEMPTS TO CURE YOU, AND I WILL SEE TO IT THAT SHE LIVES.
DECIDE.
I WANT YOU TO REALIZE THAT IN DOING THIS, I AM CHOOSING YOUR WELL-BEING OVER THAT OF THE ENTIRE EMPIRE—
BUT YOU ARE, AFTER ALL, MY SON.
I WOULD HATE TO HAVE ALL THE WORK I HAVE PUT INTO RAISING YOU WASTED.
BEFORE, YOU SAID SHE HAD TO DIE.
NOW, YOU SAY YOU'LL LET HER LIVE?
WHY?
THIS INCONSISTENCY IS UNLIKE YOU, FATHER.
WHAT ARE YOU REALLY AFTER?
AT THIS POINT, DO YOU REALLY THINK YOU CAN EVEN GET TO HER?
OH— THAT?
YES, THE FIELD IS A MESS, ISN'T IT?

HERE WE *GO*, PEOPLE, ORDERS FROM THE BARON!

ALL PHANTASMAGORICS AND MISDIRECTION UNITS, ***DISENGAGE AND FALL BACK!***

WHAT—LOOK! THE BATTLEFIELD! HOW—HOW DID THEY ***HIDE ALL THAT?***

IT WAS A ***TRICK***. AN ***AMAZING*** TRICK, BUT THE BARON HAS SOME ***AMAZING PEOPLE.***

THEY MUST ALREADY HAVE HAD ***US*** SURROUNDED—

AND WERE JUST ***WAITING*** FOR ***THESE FOOLS*** TO SHOW THEMSELVES.

VOT—
DESE GUYS?
DER BARON'S SPYMASTERS IZ FINDINK PLOTS AGAINST DE EMPIRE ALL DE TIME!
VY VOULD HE HOLD OFF ON CEPTURING OUR HETERODYNE FOR A BONCH OF GOOFS LIKE DEM?
UND LOOK OVER DERE—DOT'S THE FLYVHEEL BATTALION—DEY VOS STATIONED NEAR ISTANBUL—
IZ...IZ TOO MUCH! HE DUN NEED DIS MANY TROOPS!
DER IZ MORE TO DIS! DERE IZ SOMETING ELSE GOINK ON.

THERE. NOW, THAT'S THE TRUE SITUATION.
WHA— HOW?!
WELL?
SHALL I DESTROY HER?
YOU—YOU CAN'T!
THE CASTLE—
WE...WE REPAIRED IT...
OH, I ASSURE YOU, I CAN.
THE CASTLE YOU HAVE SUCH HOPES FOR IS DEAD.
YOU MAY HAVE REPAIRED ITS MECHANISMS,
BUT ALL THESE YEARS OF NEGLECT, FOLLOWED BY THE RECENT BURST OF ACTIVITY HAVE LEFT IT DRAINED OF MOTIVE POWER.
ACCORDING TO OUR MOST RECENT REPORTS, EVEN ITS MOST MINOR FUNCTIONS HAVE CEASED.
IT CAN NO LONGER PROTECT ITSELF, THE GIRL, OR ANYTHING ELSE.
YOU ARE NOT A FOOL. LOOK AT THE FIELD. SURELY YOU CAN SEE THAT THIS FIGHT IS OVER.
...
THE ONLY QUESTION IS: WILL THE GIRL LIVE OR DIE? CHOOSE.
ALL RIGHT! ALL RIGHT! FINE!
DON'T KILL HER!
I'LL DO ANYTHING YOU WANT!
VERY GOOD.
THERE IS... HOPE FOR YOU, YET.

ATTENTION! MECHANICSBURG IS ABOUT TO BE DESTROYED!
ALL CITIZENS ARE TO EVACUATE BY THE SOUTH GATES IMMEDIATELY.
BOOM! BOOM!
GENERAL! DEY IZ VALKING SHELLS DOWN DE NORTH ROAD!
BIG VUNS!
DER VALLS VILL NOT SCHTAND!
THEY'RE JUST GOING TO ROLL OVER US FROM NORTH TO SOUTH?!
DOTS VOT IT LOOK LIKE.
BUT— BUT WHY NOT JUST DESTROY THE WHOLE TOWN AT ONCE?
WHY DRAW IT OUT LIKE THIS?
HY TINK DEY IZ STILL HOPINK TO KETCH HYU.
OH.
YES. OF COURSE.
WELL THEN, THAT'S...
THAT'S THE BARON'S MISTAKE—AND MY CHANCE.
I CAN'T WAIT FOR THOSE GENERATORS ANY MORE. WHERE IS—
YOU WILL COME WITH US.

YOU ARE THE HETERODYNE. YOU WILL COME WITH US.
YEEK!
DREEN!
WHAT NOW?
RUN! DER BARON IZ NOT FOOLINK AROUND ENNY MORE!
DOZE TINGS IZ UNSCHTOPPABLE! VORSE—DEY'S SCARY!
REALLY REALLY SCARY!
AND REALLY REALLY STRONG!
YOU WILL COME WITH US.
NO.
CRASH!

THOOF
CLACK
LADY HETERODYNE. WOULD THAT WE HAD MET UNDER BETTER CIRCUMSTANCES.
I, MARTELLUS VON BLITZENGAARD, BY THE GRACE OF GOD AND THE VOICE OF EUROPA, AM THE NEWLY-ASCENDED STORM KING.
COME WITH ME, QUICKLY—
I WILL TAKE YOU TO SAFETY.
THE STORM KING?! BUT—
TWEEDLE, YOU IDIOT!
GET OUT OF THERE! YOU'LL BE KILLED!
tch. TARVEK.
GIVE IT UP, COUSIN. WHATEVER PATHETIC WEBS OF INTRIGUE YOU ARE CURRENTLY SPINNING ARE IN TATTERS.
YOU'VE BEEN REPLACED.
JUST SHUT UP AND JUMP! NOW!
WHOOP!
CRUMPF!
WHAT ARE YOU—
OH.
CRIK
CRUNK
YOU WILL COME WITH US.

EVERYONE, HEAD FOR THE CATHEDRAL!
GENERAL— I'LL NEED GIL'S LIGHTNING STICK.
HOKAY! VE GETS IT! HYU GO!
REPLACED? BY YOU? THERE IS NO WAY I'M PUTTING UP WITH THAT!
I AM STILL THE RIGHTFUL HEIR, AND DON'T YOU FORGET IT!
YOU ARE A SNIVELING WEAKLING, AND YOU ARE SUPPOSED TO BE DEAD!
OH, I'LL JUST BET I AM. TOO BAD THAT DIDN'T WORK OUT FOR YOU.
I WAS TOLD YOU WERE DEAD WHEN I WAS CALLED HERE!
WHAT? WHO WOULD CALL YOU?
YOUR MAJESTY! AT LAST, YOU ARRIVE!
LADY HETERODYNE! MY BLOODSTONE PALADINS STAND READY TO TAKE THEIR SWORN PLACE ALONGSIDE THE KNIGHTS OF JOVE!
OH!

LADY HETERODYNE.
I REALIZE THAT I HAVE, PERHAPS, MADE A POOR FIRST IMPRESSION.
HEY! BACK OFF, YOU PRESUMPTUOUS—
BE *SILENT*, OAF!
OBVIOUSLY THIS IS NEITHER THE TIME NOR THE PLACE FOR FLOWERY DECLARATIONS.
FOR NOW, I SHALL LET MY *ACTIONS* SPEAK FOR ME.
I HOPE THEY WILL SERVE AS A PROPER INTRODUCTION FOR LATER, WHEN WE MAY SAY ALL WE WISH.
HUP!
LOOK SHARP, LACKEY!
WHA—
AND NOW, MY LADY, IN YOUR NAME I GO—TO THRASH THE BARON'S PUPPETS *MOST SOUNDLY!*
PALADINS—*CHARGE!*
...HE'S GOING TO BE ALL *KINDS* OF TROUBLE, ISN'T HE?
WELL, *YES.* OF COURSE.

TWEEDLE'S GOOD IN A FIGHT, BUT HE JUST DOESN'T HAVE THE FIREPOWER—
AND THESE CLANKS ARE GOOD WORK, BUT THEY'RE OLD.
ALL THEY'LL DO IS BUY US SOME TIME, AND NOT MUCH OF THAT.
I KNOW!
COME ON. WE NEED TO GET CLOSER TO THE CASTLE. SOMEPLACE AS HIGH AS POSSIBLE.

YOU ARE GOING NOWHERE.
WHOA!

DO NOT COMMIT THE FOLLY OF BELIEVING YOURSELF A TRUE HETERODYNE, YOUNG LADY.
YOU MAY HAVE TRICKED A BROKEN CASTLE INTO ACCEPTING YOU,

BUT WE BOTH KNOW THAT YOU ARE NOTHING BUT A PAWN TO HELP SMOOTH THE ASCENSION OF THE STORM KING.
YOU WILL COME WITH ME TO THE CATACOMBS,
WHERE YOU WILL BE KEPT SAFE UNTIL YOU ARE NEEDED. NOW—

CLONG!
TRUST ME.
YOU WOULDN'T GET ANYWHERE TRYING TO ARGUE WITH HER.
YOU REALLY ARE THE BEST MINION EVER.
I AM NOT HER MINION!
TELL HIM! TELL HIM I'M NOT YOUR MINION!
HE'S NOT MY MINION.

DOES HE SERIOUSLY BELIEVE THAT?
I THINK IT'S SOMETHING LIKE WISHFUL THINKING.
...WELL, MAYBE MORE LIKE HOPEFUL SHOUTING.
—SOMEWHERE WHERE SHE WON'T CAUSE ANY TROUBLE!
TCH. KIDS TODAY—DON'T EVEN RECOGNIZE THEIR HETERODYNE... SHOCKING.
KNOW WHAT I BLAME? I BLAME THAT NEW DANCE MUSIC—
IF YOU CAN CALL IT THAT.
HEH. POLKA DOTTY, I CALLS IT.
HO! GOOD ONE!
HO DERE, SVEETHOT! DE GENERAL SEZ HYU NEEDS HYU ZAPPY STICK!
GUYS! THANK GOODNESS!
I WAS AFRAID IT MIGHT BE BROKEN.
...AND WHAT ARE YOU PLANNING TO DO WITH THAT?
THE CASTLE NEEDS A LOT OF POWER, FAST—
SO I'M GOING TO USE THIS TO HIT IT WITH A BIG BOLT OF LIGHTNING!
AAAAH! NOT HERE! NOT HERE!
OF COURSE I'M NOT GOING TO DO IT HERE.
YOU WANT TO, THOUGH, DON'T YOU?
I CAN TELL!
...IRRELEVANT. I NEED TO GET A LOT CLOSER TO THE CASTLE.
I'M THINKING THE HETERODYNE'S OBSERVATION TOWER.
OOH! NIZE CHOICE!
THIS PLACE—IT'S REALLY HIGH UP, RIGHT?
HO, YEZ!
IN A LIGHTNING STORM.
HYU BETCHA!
...I KNEW IT.

LET ME GUESS. THAT REALLY TALL ONE? WAY OVER THERE?
WELL, YES...
YOU'LL NEVER MAKE IT.
"LISTEN. THE CASTLE'S HAD ME RUNNING ALL OVER TOWN MAKING REPAIRS."
"THE BARON IS DESTROYING EVERYTHING!"
"THERE ARE CLANKS EVERYWHERE. THEY'RE ROUNDING PEOPLE UP AND HERDING THEM TOWARD THE SOUTH GATE.
...AND EVEN IF YOU COULD AVOID ALL THE FIRE, EXPLOSIONS AND CLANKS—"
"THE ENTIRE PLACE IS BEING OVERRUN WITH WULFENBACH TROOPS—PLUS WHAT HAS GOT TO BE EVERY SPARK, CONSTRUCT AND RANDOM ABOMINATION THE BARON HAS!
THIS TOWN IS FINISHED!
ALL WE CAN DO IS TRY TO FIND A WAY OUT OF HERE BEFORE WE'RE KILLED!"
BUT...YOU SAY NOBODY CAN GET THROUGH ALL THAT...
THERE'S JUST NO WAY!
AND YOU'VE BEEN DOING WORK ALL OVER TOWN!
THAT'S RIGHT! SO I'VE SEEN IT! IT'S HOPELESS!
HO! HYU IZ VUN HECKUVA USEFUL GUY!
HYU COME VIT US!
YAH! VE GETS DERE FOR SURE IF VE BRINGS HYU ALONG!
NOOOOO!
YOU'D THINK HE'D LEARN.
HEH! DE BEST MINIONS NEFFER DO!

HEH. BUT EVEN VIT MEESTER EXPERT GUIDE, VE IZ STILL GUN HAFF TROUBLE GEDDING OVER DERE.
KEN HYU USE DOT LIGHTNING SCHTICK TO CLEAR A PATH?
NO. IT'S FRAGILE. IF I USE IT TOO MUCH I COULD BURN IT OUT—
OR EVEN WORSE, WASTE THE ATMOSPHERIC IONIZATION ENGINES THAT PRODUCE THE BIG CHARGE I'M GOING TO NEED.
ZO—HYU IZ NEW...VOT HEPPEN TO DE ODDER SCHMOT GUY, HEY?
HE...WELL... I DON'T KNOW.
I...THINK THAT'S GOING TO DEPEND ON HOW SMART A GUY HE REALLY IS.
...UND VOT ABOUT HYU, HEY?
hmf. SO IZ WORSE DEN USELESS.
NOT ONLY KEN VE NOT USE IT, VE GOTS TO PROTECT IT.
OH... THAT'S TRUE...
ALL RIGHT THEN. I'LL IMPROVE IT.
I'LL BET THERE ARE ALL KINDS OF THINGS I CAN DO TO MAKE IT STRONGER.
...AS VE IZ FIGHTING THROUGH A VAR ZONE?
IF I CAN GET THE PARTS ALONG THE WAY, SURE.
VELL, DOT VILL BE NO PROBLEM!
HY BETS DIS GUY KNOWS VERE VE KEN GETS ALL KINDS OV GOOT SCHTUFF!
NOOOO!
YOU KNOW, WE COULD JUST CHUCK IT ALL AND TURN TO PIRACY.
IT'D BE A LOT EASIER.
HOY! HE IZ A SCHMOT GUY!

SOON—
KA-BOOM! FOOM!
SHREEEEEEEEEE!
AAUGH! LOOKIT DOT!
WHAT?! WHAT IS IT?!
DEY TURN MY FAVORIT GRIND-HYU-OWN-SAUSAGE BAR INTO A SCHTUPID FLOWER SHOP!
DOT IZ A CRIME, DOT IZ!
WILL YOU PLEASE STOP DOING THAT!
QVIET. KEEP BECK.
DIMO?
IZ VUN OV DE BARON'S PHLOGISTON POWERED MANTIGOONS.
HE GOTS DEM OFF OL' PROFESSOR PONGLENOZE LAST YEAR.
DEY'LL BURN ANYTING TO A LEEDLE CRISP!
J&J mire mead
PONGLE— PROFESSOR WUBERTUS PONGLENOZE?
UH, MEYBE? HY TINK SO...
DOCTOR BEETLE SAID PONGLENOZE DEVELOPED A BRILLIANT INTERLOCK SYSTEM FOR REGULATING ENERGY SYSTEMS!
OH! I READ ABOUT THAT!
SUPPOSEDLY IT IMPROVES SWITCH EFFICIENCY BY A FACTOR OF FIVE!
HMM...
CAN YOU GUYS...GET IT FOR ME?
WHOO! YAH! VE HUNT!
WAIT! NO!
NOT ME! WHY ME?!
HEY, SOMEVUN GOTS TO TELL US VOT AN INTER-VOTCHUMACALLIT LOOKS LIKE!

AND SO—
VHOOHOO! VE GOTS *ANODDER VUN!*
HOO, NOW! HY VOS PREDDY IMPRESSED VEN HYU HIT DER DRIVER VIT DOT *BRICK!*
WELL— GOING FOR THE WEAKEST PART GETS THE FIGHT OVER *QUICK!*
SEE—*DOT'S* DE PART HY DUN UNNERSTAND...
THERE! HOW ABOUT *THAT?!*
YEAH! HEY, YOU KNOW WHAT *THIS* NEEDS?
SOME SORT OF PHASE-LOCK MULTIPLIER!
OOH! *NOW* YOU'RE TALKING!
BUT WHERE WOULD WE FIND-
HOY! VOT IZ HYU KEEDS DOINK HERE?
DERE IZ A SQVAD OV *BLOATER TANKS* COMINK DIS VAY!
VE IZ ON OUR VAY TO *MEETS* DEM!
YAH!
BLOATER TANKS?
ARE THEY THE KIND FEATURED IN BARON VON TWANGSNEKKEN'S BOOK:
TWENTY-SEVEN AMUSING THOUGHTS ON URBAN WARFARE AND AFTER-DINNER MINTS?!
ERM—
DEY GOTS BEEG *GONZ* ON DEM...
GOOD ENOUGH!
HERE. THE PARTS I WANT LOOK LIKE *THIS.*
THANK YOU!
THANK YOU!
HMM! HOKAY, BOYS—
LEZ GO *SHOPPINK!*

EVENTUALLY—
-SO YOU SEE WHAT I'M GOING FOR?
OF COURSE. BUT IT'S NOT QUITE-
I KNOW, BUT I CAN'T FIGURE OUT WHAT IT STILL NEEDS...
I KNOW WHAT IT NEEDS!
OTHAR!
WHAT ARE YOU DOING HERE?
IT NEEDS ONE OF THOSE-
AH, ONE OF THOSE-
OH, HOW EMBARRASSING. IT'S GONE COMPLETELY OUT OF MY HEAD.
HOLD ON.
HUP!
!
OOF!
SMASH!
RRRIP!
BASH!
Rummage Rummage
YOU KNOW, ONE OF THESE!
OH! RIGHT! THAT'S PERFECT!
I...KEEP FORGETTING HE'S A SPARK.
REALLY. SO YOU'VE COMPLETELY MISSED THE FAC THAT HE'S OVERBEARING,
SELF-AGGRANDIZING AND CERTAIN DEATH TO BE AROUND?
WELL, NO,
YOUR POINT?

OH, YES! YES, YES, YES!
IT IS SOOO READY! HEE HEE HEE!
um...YEAH, THAT OUGHT TO DO IT.
...OR YOU COULD JUST BLOW CASTLE WULFENBACH OUT OF THE SKY...
AN EXCELLENT SUGGESTION, YOUNG APPRENTICE!
urgh. EXCEPT GIL IS STILL UP THERE—
ooh! EVEN BETTER!
AND HE'S STILL GOT MY NOTES. SO, NO.
VERRA NIZE! UND VOT HYU VANTS VE DO NEXT?
IT'S TIME TO HEAD FOR THE OBSERVATION TOWER!
VELL, HOKAY... BUT DERE IZ SCHTILL ALL DOSE CLENKS UND TINGS IN DE VAY—
I DON'T THINK THAT'S GOING TO BE A PROBLEM NOW.
VUM VUM VUM
CRACKLE
WATCH THIS!
BZZZAKK!

KRAZZOWN!
BTHAM!
K-K-K-
RRKKK-K
FLOOOM!
...HOW IS IT *POSSIBLE* THAT THIS COULD SURPRISE *ANY* OF YOU PEOPLE?

UM...DO WE HAVE ANY OTHER TALL BUILDINGS NEAR THE CASTLE?
—THAT YOU'RE NOT TOO ATTACHED TO?
HO, VERRA NIZE! VERRA NIZE!
YEZ! NIZE SHOT!
OH, SURE! HOW ABOUT THE CATHEDRAL SPIRE?!
OR THE DOOM BELL!
HMM...NOT HIGH ENOUGH... NOT CLOSE ENOUGH...
I'M NOT SERIOUS!
VELL, COULDN'T HYU JUST RUN AROUND ZAPPING EFFRYTING VIT DOT SCHITCK?
YOU'D BETTER NOT BE SERIOUS!
I'D RUN OUT OF CHARGE LONG BEFORE I GOT THEM ALL,
THE POINT IS TO SAVE THE TOWN, NOT FLATTEN IT—
AND THE CASTLE WOULD STILL BE DEAD.
WELL, IF ALTITUDE IS ALL YOU NEED,
YOUNG WULFENBACH HAS HELPFULLY PROVIDED US WITH A FLYING MACHINE!
'TWOULD BE SO VERY TRÈS IRONIC!
NEVER MENTION THAT BUCKET OF BOLTS IN MY PRESENCE EVER AGAIN.
DOES THE LADY HETERODYNE NEED TO GO FLYING?

I CAN FLY YOU HIGHER AND CLOSER THAN ANY BUILDING IN TOWN!
FRANZ!
THAT WOULD BE PERFECT!
WHAT?!
FRANZ, YOU CAN'T FLY!
BUT—
I CAN TOO FLY.
HE CAN'T!
I CAN!
I JUST...
YOU KNOW...
CHEAT A

IT'S WONDERFUL!
...AND I THINK YOU FLY VERY WELL.
HA! YEAH! MASTER BARRY MADE IT FOR ME!
HE SAID ALL THE STUFF WITH THE BIRDS AND KITES WAS JUST SILLY.
SO, HOW CLOSE DO WE NEED TO GET?

I'M NOT SURE... BUT...
SINCE WE'RE ALREADY IN THE AIR, CAN'T WE JUST LAND RIGHT ON THE ROOF?
OH, SURE. TERRIFIC. *WHY NOT?*
OH? WHAT'S WRONG?
NOTHING... ASIDE FROM THE FACT THAT THE LONGER WE'RE UP HERE, THE BETTER OUR CHANCES OF GETTING BLOWN OUT OF THE SKY.
BUT HEY, NO PROBLEM. THE ROOF IT IS.
FRANZ... UM...
HOW LONG HAVE YOU SERVED THE HETERODYNES?
EH. A PRETTY LONG TIME. 'COUPLE HUNDRED YEARS, I THINK...
I LOSE TRACK WHEN I'M SLEEPING.
WHY?
WELL, IT'S JUST...
WELL, IS THIS GOING TO *WORK?*
HUH? WHAT DO YOU MEAN?
I MEAN TRYING TO GIVE IT A JOLT LIKE THIS.
THOSE THINGS UP THERE LOOK LIKE COLLECTORS TO ME,
BUT IS THAT *REALLY* WHAT THEY ARE? AND IS THE CASTLE *STRONG* ENOUGH?
HUH.
JEEZ. I DUNNO, I'VE NEVER SEEN IT *THIS* BAD.
YOU'RE THE HETERODYNE. ALL THAT TECHNICAL STUFF IS UP TO *YOU.*
HEH. IF NOTHING ELSE, IT'LL KEEP 'EM BUSY WHILE YOU MAKE YOUR ESCAPE!

ESCAPE?
YOU MEAN, RUN AWAY?!
WELL, YEAH. OF COURSE.
I WON'T—
WHY NOT? TOO PROUD?
YOU COULD GIVE 'EM A GOOD RANT BEFORE YOU RUN, YOU KNOW.
LOTS OF HETERODYNES HAVE DONE IT.
THEY WERE ALWAYS GETTING BEAT BACK, THWARTED, FOILED—
'S WHY YOU RULE MECHANICSBURG AND NOT THE WORLD.
SOMETIMES YOU JUST GOTTA KNOW WHEN TO SET A FEW TIME-DELAYED DEATH-TRAPS AND RUN.
REBUILD YOUR POWER.
SHOW 'EM ALL ANOTHER DAY.
IT HAPPENS.
I...I CAN'T DO THAT.
THE OLD HETERODYNES... MY ANCESTORS... WHENEVER THEY WERE BEATEN BACK, THEY CAME HERE.
NO ONE COULD TAKE MECHANICSBURG. THAT WAS THEIR STRENGTH.
IF I RUN AWAY AND LOSE MECHANICSBURG, I—WE—HAVE NOWHERE TO RUN TO.
...
NOTRE DAME'S MAYBE GOT OPENINGS IN THE GARGOYLE SQUAD...?
KEEP FLYING!

OH, YES... THOSE THINGS ARE DEFINITELY NOT JUST THERE FOR DECORATION.
LAND ME NEAR THE ONE ON THE FAR LEFT.
(HUFF) YEAH, YEAH! (HUFF) BE CAREFUL, NOW–THAT ROOF'S PROBABLY SLIPPERY, AND WE CAN'T BE SURE IT'LL HOLD OUR (HUFF) WEIGHT.
RIGHT.
WELL, IF THE MASTERS WEREN'T HERE...
AND THE CASTLE NEVER SAID ANYTHING...
SO—IF THESE ARE COLLECTORS,
THEY CAN'T BE WORKING RIGHT.
THE CASTLE MUST GET HIT BY LIGHTNING ONCE IN A WHILE...
OHHH! SEE? AFTER THEY GOT HIT, THESE CONNECTIONS SHOULD HAVE RESET!
I'LL BET THEY GOT TRIPPED YEARS AGO. BUT...NO ONE EVER CHECKED?
THERE! THAT SHOULD DO IT!
hmf! SEE? IT'S A GOOD THING THAT TOWER COLLAPSED...
AGATHA!

GIL!
YOU'RE ALL RIGHT!
COME ABOARD! QUICKLY!
YOU'VE DONE YOUR BEST—
BUT THE TOWN HAS FALLEN. IT'S OVER.
I'M GETTING YOU OUT OF HERE!
NO— HOLD ON, I—
WHOOP!
AAAAAAAAH!
AGATHA!
OOF!

AH! BE CAREFUL!
HOLD STILL. I'LL BE RIGHT THERE.
WHOA THERE. HOLD ON, YOU.
SHE'S OKAY–I'VE GOT HER.
HUH.
CAREFUL, M'LADY–
SOMETHING AIN'T RIGHT WITH THIS GUY.
C'MERE, KID. LET ME HAVE A BETTER LOOK AT YA.
CHOK
STAY BACK!
OW!
WHATTA YOU THINK... UH...
FWHUMP!
FRANZ!
OOOG!
GIL! WHAT'VE YOU DONE TO HIM?!
HE WASN'T GOING TO HURT YOU!
HE'S ONE OF MINE!
IT'S ONLY A SEDATIVE. HE'LL BE FINE.
BUT I DON'T HAVE TIME TO ARGUE WITH HIM–
OR YOU. COME WITH ME!
NOW!
OH, NO–
YOU STAY WHERE YOU ARE.

STAY-YOU CAN'T BE SERIOUS!
THE STORM IS GETTING WORSE! WE CAN'T STAY UP HERE!
YES! FINE! GET YOURSELF DOWN TO THE TOWN SQUARE.
FIND TARVEK AND VAN. YOU CAN HELP THEM AND BE OUT OF THE STORM.
I'LL TALK TO YOU WHEN I'M DONE HERE-
AGATHA, YOU'VE GOT TO LISTEN TO REASON!
THIS HAS GONE TOO FAR!
NO. NOT YET. I'M NOT FINISHED HERE.
I HAVEN'T GIVEN UP-
AND I AM NOT LEAVING THIS TOWN!
THE TOWN? LOOK AT IT! THIS TOWN IS IN FLAMES!
IF THIS KEEPS UP, ALL OF EUROPA WILL BE LIKE THIS!
I'VE EXPLAINED EVERYTHING TO MY FATHER!
HE UNDERSTANDS! HE CAN HELP YOU!
IF YOU KEEP TRYING TO SOLVE THIS BY YOURSELF, THE OTHER WILL WIN, AND WE'LL BE BACK TO THE DAYS OF CONSTANT WARFARE!
DIDN'T YOU HEAR ME? MECHANICSBURG HAS FALLEN! WHAT ELSE DO YOU THINK YOU CAN DO?
KRAKK
THIS!

BOOOM!

TO BE CONTINUED IN:

GIRL GENIUS® Book THIRTEEN

KEEP UP WITH THE STORY! READ NEW COMICS THREE TIMES A WEEK AT:

WWW.GIRLGENIUS.NET

© P P Foglio -10
Kaja

MEANWHILE, AT TRANSYLVANIA POLYGNOSTIC UNIVERSITY—
GREAT GOOGLY-MOOGLY! THE 2013 HUGO NOMINATIONS ARE OUT!
YEAH, AND WE'RE NOT ONE OF THEM!
YOU CLAIMED THIS DEVICE COULD BE REPAIRED!
LIES!
LOCUS
ANNUAL SFWA SWIMSUIT ISSUE
MIND CONTROL ENGINE
ON
THIS IS GREAT!
HOW EXACTLY IS THIS GREAT? WE WERE ONLY SUPPOSED TO SIT OUT ONE YEAR!
DON'T YOU SEE? IT MEANS WE'VE SHOWN THEM, SHOWN THEM ALL!
BUT... MY MECHANICAL HUGO-NAUT...
I HAVEN'T EVEN UNLEASHED IT YET...
THE BEST GRAPHIC STORY CATEGORY IS REALLY NEW, AND WE WON THE FIRST THREE!
SO SOME PEOPLE SAID THERE WAS NO POINT TO THE AWARD, SINCE WE'D JUST KEEP WINNING IT—
WHICH WAS ACTUALLY PRETTY NICE OF THEM—
BUT JUST LOOK AT ALL THE GREAT WORKS BEING HONORED THIS YEAR!
CONGRATULATIONS, EVERYBODY!
GRANDVILLE BÊTE NOIRE
written and illustrated by Bryan Talbot
(Dark Horse Comics, Jonathan Cape)
LOCKE & KEY VOLUME 5: CLOCKWORKS
written by Joe Hill, illustrated by Gabriel Rodriguez
(IDW)
SAGA, VOLUME ONE
written by Brian K. Vaughn, illustrated by Fiona Staples
(Image Comics)
SCHLOCK MERCENARY: RANDOM ACCESS MEMORABILIA
WWW.SCHLOCKMERCENARY.COM
by Howard Tayler, colors by Travis Walton
(Hypernode Media)
SAUCER COUNTRY, VOLUME 1: RUN
written by Paul Cornell, illustrated by Ryan Kelly, Jimmy Broxton and Goran Sudžuka
(Vertigo)
AND, MY MINIONS, REMEMBER THIS WELL:
ALL YOU MUST DO TO BE ELIGIBLE TO VOTE IS BE A MEMBER OF THE WORLD SCIENCE FICTION CONVENTION!
THIS YEAR, IT'S LONESTARCON 3 IN SAN ANTONIO!
COME FOR THE ALAMO, STAY FOR THE BATS!
WELL... AS LONG AS I GET BARBECUE...
WAIT-
DID HE SAY "BATS?"
WWW.LONESTARCON3.ORG

MAIDEN

Girl Genius® ©2013 Studio Foglio LLC • www.girlgenius.net • Drawing by Phil Foglio, Color by Cheyenne Wrig

C. WRIGHT
©P. FOGLIO-11
ONWARD!

YAH, YAH, SO I OVERSLEPT.
HAPPY NEW YEAR, ALREADY.

READ MORE COMICS ONLINE AT:
WWW.GIRLGENIUS.NET
MONDAY · WEDNESDAY · FRIDAY